THE OPPOSITE OF EMPTY

Your Guide to the Purpose Activation Blueprint

IZABELA OQUENDO

LANDON HAIL PRESS

Copyright© 2025 Izabela Oquendo
All Rights Reserved

This book or any portion thereof may not be reproduced or used in any manner without the express written permission of the publisher, except for the use of brief quotations in a book review.

Paperback ISBN: 978-1-959955-64-1
Hardback ISBN: 978-1-959955-65-8

Cover design by Rich Johnson, Spectacle Photo
Published by Landon Hail Press

Although the author and publisher have made every effort to ensure the accuracy and completeness of information contained in this book, we assume no responsibility for errors, inaccuracies, omissions, or any inconsistency herein. Any slights on people, places, or organizations are unintentional. The material in this book is provided for educational purposes only. No responsibility for loss occasioned to any person or corporate body acting or refraining to act as a result of reading material in this book can be accepted by the author or publisher.

To my late father, who always pushed me to be the best, I hope I have made you proud. You made me who I am today, and I'm eternally grateful for the grit and resilience you instilled in me. My guardian angel, my protector, please watch over us as we continue on this beautiful, crazy journey.

And to my mother, my soft spot, my continuous supporter. You've watched me take major risks in my life, and although I know I've made you lose sleep at night, you've allowed me the space to grow and expand. For that, I am thankful.

You both came to the United States in search of the American Dream, to start a better life for us, and I'm proud to report: you succeeded. You laid the foundation for everything that I am and everything that I've accomplished. I commend you for your bravery, leaving everything behind to start over in a foreign place, and now I will follow in your footsteps.

CONTENTS

FOREWORD _____ 1
INTRODUCTION _____ 5
   Fulfillment _____ 6
   How I Did It _____ 8
   Why Purpose Matters _____ 20
   What to Expect from the Process _____ 25
   The Purpose Activation Blueprint Approach _____ 30
CHAPTER 1: The Foundations of Purpose _____ 34
   Common Misconceptions _____ 36
   Beginning Your Purpose Activation Blueprint _____ 38
CHAPTER 2: The Power of Self-Awareness _____ 42
   Introspection _____ 44
   Identifying Your Core Beliefs _____ 45
   Chapter 2 Exploration Exercises _____ 48
CHAPTER 3: Uncovering Your Authentic Values ___ 50
   What Values Mean _____ 51
   The Origin of Values _____ 52
   Chapter 3 Exploration Exercises _____ 58
CHAPTER 4: Tapping into Your Unique Talents and Strengths _____ 60

Leveraging Strengths in Your Purpose _____ 61

Hard vs. Soft Skills _____ 63

Developing Soft Skills _____ 65

Chapter 4 Exploration Exercises _____ 73

CHAPTER 5: Passion as a Compass _____ 75

Defining Passion _____ 75

Flow State _____ 78

Intrinsic vs. Extrinsic Motivation _____ 79

Chapter 5 Exploration Exercises _____ 85

CHAPTER 6: The Impact of Life Experiences _____ 87

Subconscious Reprogramming _____ 88

Turning Pain Into Purpose _____ 95

Chapter 6 Exploration Exercises _____ 101

CHAPTER 7: Understanding Your Needs _____ 104

Preferences for Productivity _____ 105

Personality as an Indicator of Needs _____ 106

Needs and Purpose _____ 109

Exploring the Needs of Your Past Self _____ 113

Chapter 7: Exploration Exercises _____ 115

CHAPTER 8: The Intersection of Purpose and Service _ 117

Service to Others _____ 117

Purpose Beyond the Self _____ 119

Mindful Manifest Flow _____ 124

Releasing Self-Interest _____ 126

- Purpose Evolution ... 130
- Chapter 8 Exploration Exercises ... 134
- CHAPTER 9: Overcoming Fear and Doubt ... 136
  - The True Nature of Fear ... 137
  - Fears and Purpose ... 139
  - Fear of Failure ... 142
  - How to Embody Your Higher Self ... 147
  - Fear of What Others Will Think ... 150
  - Fear of Not Being Enough ... 154
  - Fear of What Will Change ... 159
  - Fear of Letting Go of the Facade ... 170
  - The Common Denominator of Fear ... 171
- CHAPTER 10: Designing Your Purpose Activation Blueprint ... 176
  - Creating your Blueprint ... 177
  - Purpose in Action ... 183
  - Surrendering to Your Purpose ... 187
- CHAPTER 11: Sustaining Purpose Over Time ... 191
  - Evolving Purpose ... 191
  - Reflection Prompt: Revisiting Your Career Path Through the Lens of Purpose ... 201
  - How to Know You're on the Right Track ... 202
  - Staying Aligned ... 204
  - Celebrating Milestones ... 212
  - Final Reflections ... 216

SOURCE NOTES	222
ACKNOWLEDGMENTS	223
ABOUT THE AUTHOR	225

FOREWORD

WHEN I FIRST MET Izabela Oquendo, I was immediately inspired by her authenticity. It's a rare and contagious quality that draws you in and makes you feel seen. We met on an introduction call with the publishing team I work with, guiding aspiring writers through the intimidating process of bringing their stories to life. Izabela stood out, not just for her bubbly personality but also for her tireless desire to help women expand into their full potential. Her passion for empowering others and her voice were something I knew instantly the world needed to hear. That meeting was the first of many on her publishing journey, which has inspired me deeply and led to this amazing book you now hold, *The Opposite of Empty*.

As an author coach, I've had the privilege of working with many writers, each with their own unique vision and story to tell. But Izabela's project felt different from the start. Her book is a blueprint for discovering your purpose and summoning the grit to pursue it—an idea that has driven much of my own life.

I've always believed that where we are today isn't where we always have to be, and that, within us, there's an urge for something greater, a pull toward a life that aligns with our true purpose. Following those little nudges and developing the discipline to act on them has transformed my life and led me toward my own purpose. To read Izabela's words and know that she communicates the same belief with such clarity and conviction was nothing short of breathtaking.

As she worked on her manuscript, I had the privilege of getting an early peek at *The Opposite of Empty*. I couldn't put it down. I read it on flights, in my living room, and on my phone as I ran errands. Page after page, I was drawn into her stories–raw, vulnerable, and relatable. Her willingness to share her own struggles, emotions, and secrets with such openness resonated deeply with me. The stories she wrote didn't feel like just her own; they are universal, reflecting the fears and dreams of women everywhere. I found myself nodding along, drawn in by the honesty she shared and inspired by the reality she created.

Izabela has completely changed her own life, transforming challenges and discomfort in the *norm* into stepping stones toward a vision she had the desire to create through faith in her purpose. I believe her impact is just beginning. She has helped countless women rediscover their own paths, empowering them to step into their lives filled with meaning and purpose. I've witnessed the ripple effect of her work – women inspired to take bold steps, to trust their inner voices, and to build lives that allow them to feel alive.

The Opposite of Empty is more than a book; it's a blueprint. Izabela asks you to listen to those subtle inner whispers, the ones that hint at a bigger, more fulfilling life. You won't read this book and wonder where to begin. She provides a roadmap, equipping you with the tools to uncover your purpose and the resilience to follow it, no matter what obstacles are in front of you. Her guidance is grounded in her own experiences and guided by her desire to see every woman step fully into her purpose.

This book will ask you to look within, to confront your fears, and to allow yourself to live a life of purpose. It will also remind you that you're not alone on this journey. You'll connect with every story, every season, and every emotion as she guides you toward a life that is bigger, bolder, and more meaningful.

The shift you're looking for, the craving for something more, it's waiting, and *The Opposite of Empty* is your guide to claiming it.

>Raina O'Dell, Best-Selling Author of *BARE: An Unveiling of my Naked Truth*
>Writing & Publishing Coach with Landon Hail Press
>Writing & Riding Retreat Host

INTRODUCTION

THE OPPOSITE OF EMPTY is full. And my intention for this book is to leave you feeling full—full of purpose, full of excitement, full of fulfillment in your life. I know what it's like to live with emptiness inside and how hard it is to look forward to a day-to-day experience that doesn't spark joy or excitement. It's exhausting to live the same day over and over again. So many people do this and call it a life.

My aim is to help you transform that emptiness and shift from monotony to enthusiasm. I'm going to help you make that shift by introducing you to a process I, myself, have used to spark joy and create the life of my absolute dreams. I love what I do now, so I no longer dread my work. My weekends are thoroughly enjoyed because the Sunday Scaries never creep up, and I look forward to the week ahead. I feel in control of my work and my life. I don't avoid people who bring me down, because I only associate with those who light me up, and I get to say "yes" to every single thing I want to do because I've created freedom in my life that allows me to live on my terms. I went from living anxiously, overwhelmed and paycheck to paycheck, to a life full of adventure and wonder and vibrancy.

I want nothing more than to share this process with you so that you, too, can change your life. I want you to experience the joy, the thrill, and the sheer exhilaration we're supposed to feel. This is not a way of life reserved for the privileged; it is available to anyone and everyone. You just need to be bold enough to make the changes necessary to shift into this new state of existence. And I'm here to teach you how.

I hope this process is as life-changing for you as it was for me. The beautiful thing about change is that it compounds. Once you take the first step toward truly shifting your mindset and moving closer to living your purpose, you will see just how quickly things unfold. When you begin to align with your purpose, you will find that you are exactly where you are meant to be and things will suddenly start making sense.

It's like falling into orbit. Once you step into the gravitational field of your true purpose, you are shown exactly where to go next. Things become easy, and they begin to flow naturally. There is no more resistance. There is only alignment. It's a beautiful, wonderful feeling to align with your purpose, and I'm here to help you step into yours.

Fulfillment

I've yet to meet someone who has lived a happy life without first hitting a significant low point. Maybe not rock bottom per se, although that may look different for different people, but somewhere well below neutral. Happy is a relative term, and it can only be felt when the person has experienced something counter to it. You have to experience your version of unhappiness to truly appreciate happiness. I know there are various meanings to the word, so for the purposes of this book we're going to call it "fulfillment."

Fulfillment can be described as a feeling of accomplishment based on purpose. This book is about purpose and how to find it, so rest assured, you will have a solid understanding of exactly what it is and where to look for it by the end of our time together.

The low point I'm referring to is pivotal in facing who you are and deciding where to go from there. It's an opportunity for transformation. When you're feeling your lowest, it's a chance to clean up your habits and change the way you're doing things. You enter a mindset of change. The key to rising high above your life as you've known it and creating joy, excitement, and fulfillment is taking advantage of the momentum of change.

You have to change anyway. To get you back on your feet, you have to change your mindset. To start functioning normally again, you have to change your habits. Rather than getting back to "normal" after a low point, you might as well continue improving yourself, riding the wave of change. For example, if you gain weight and finally decide enough is enough, you can improve your eating and exercise habits to bring you back to your normal weight, or you can continue improving yourself until you're better than you were before the gain. The same principle applies to mindset and other habits.

We all go through these low points where life just feels like it's against us. Whether it's following a loss or failure or disappointment, it can feel like things will never improve and happiness will forever be reserved for those more fortunate than us

If you've ever been there, you know how hard it is to pick yourself up from that place. It requires energy. Where do you get that energy? From a place most people don't visit as often as they should: hope.

When working through these low points, most people hope to get back to feeling normal. But what if we harnessed that momentum and hoped for better, more abundant, more successful *instead* of normal? You've got to put in the work to get back to your baseline anyway, so why not make those changes bigger and grander to catapult you beyond your normal and emerge as a higher, happier, more fulfilled version of yourself?

The low points in our lives are sacred, and everyone experiences them personally. They give us a chance to really prove ourselves and what we're capable of. The principles in this book will show you how to harness the momentum of rising from the ashes to soar higher than you ever thought possible. The simple fact that you felt compelled to read this book indicates there are areas of your life that could use some improvement. Regardless of where you are in the healing process—whether you just entered a low point or you're already on your way back to normal—you can harness the momentum of healing to bring you up to a level of happiness and fulfillment you didn't know existed for you.

How I Did It

I hit my low point when I was in my early thirties. It was the second worst I have ever felt. My first worst was my coming of age and involved a lot of drinking and self-exploration. That's a story for another day (and another book), but I will tell you that the conclusion to that phase involved a lot of soul-searching and a quest for purpose, which led me to the discovery of manifestation and the idea that our thoughts determine our outcomes.

I'm a huge introvert, so I basically live in my own head, and my thoughts are incredibly sacred to me. When I learned that my thoughts were keeping me stuck in a cycle of self-loathing, I felt betrayed. It was like finding out my best friend was sabotaging me. I retrained the voice in my head, though, to speak to me with love, compassion, and belief in my positive outcomes.

From that point, I had successfully manifested a beautiful life. I was comfortable. And from the outside, it looked like I had nothing to complain about. But on the inside, I was screaming for something new. I call this part of my life "Phase 1."

Let me paint a picture for you, so you can determine if this is someone who should be feeling unfulfilled. I was in my early thirties with two healthy kids and a loving husband, John. I had a teaching job at a university, and, in addition, I had a thriving bookkeeping business that was growing. I also had just finished getting licensed as a psychotherapist, with the intention of fully transitioning into that line of work. John also had a growing business as a home inspector. We had two brand-new cars sitting in the driveway of our beautiful 2,000-square-foot house in a nice neighborhood, right on the edge of the town where most of our friends lived. This is exactly the life I'd wanted. I'd worked hard, and I'd manifested all of this.

So, what was there to complain about? Why was I feeling unfulfilled? It's because I wasn't led there by true alignment. I searched for purpose, but I think I just wasn't ready to face myself and do an honest evaluation of who I am. I wish I'd had a book like this when I set out on my journey to guide me through the necessary work of introspection.

When I set out on my search, though, there were plenty of forces other than alignment that brought me to the place I thought I belonged. I followed some principles of purpose, like evaluating strengths, serving others, and following values. The problem, however, was that I wasn't sure of myself yet, and I also followed the desire to appear "normal" and "successful" in the way I thought it was supposed to look. I had not yet developed a solid, unshakable identity or self-concept, at this point. My values followed a pattern of what my parents believed, what was normal in society for my area and age group, and some idea of world peace that is probably not possible in this lifetime. This is why I was steered in the wrong direction. I made some impressive moves, but they did not suit my true purpose.

I was trying on many hats and trying to see which piece of spaghetti would stick to the wall. I was all over the place and mentally stretched thin because of it. I was running an internship program at a university and teaching psychology, and I also had a bookkeeping business. You might wonder how the two are connected, and they're not, no matter how much I tried to make them both part of the same identity.

My business was growing and thriving, and my intention was to replace my university income with bookkeeping, which would allow me to work entirely from home. I got to that point and then some, yet still didn't feel comfortable enough to leave my job. Very near to the low point that changed everything for me, I also became a Licensed Professional Counselor, with the intention of starting yet another business, a small psychotherapy practice. Oh! And John and I were real estate investors with several rental properties, as well.

I told you. All over the place. This is a tell-tale sign of someone who is not in alignment. Being pulled in so many different directions is hustle. We're taught that hustle is the key to success. I'm here to tell you it's not. Hustle is the key to money, and money is not equivalent to success. I do have good news for anyone who picked up this book to learn how to make money, though. Financial abundance very often flows to the person who is aligned with their purpose.

During my hustle days, I was making good money, but it felt hard. Every day was a struggle, and I dreaded my work schedule. Now, my work feels easy but impactful. I love what I do, and I look forward to it every single day. Financial abundance has certainly followed my purpose-driven work, but this time, I am holding the money in a new way. I use it to create good in the world and to spark joy in me instead of buying nice things with the intention of sparking envy from others, like I did before.

When I started my business, I planned to leave my job at the university after hitting a certain monthly income. That point came and went, and on I forged, continuing to teach. That's because the income I had in mind was no longer enough to support my ever-increasing spending. Between the time I started my business and when I hit that figure, I upgraded my house and my cars, I had another baby, and I got a pool, a new hot tub, etc. All within two years.

As the money flowed in, so it flowed out. This is a common trap set up by consumerism. We're conditioned to show off our prosperity, especially when we come from humble beginnings. I've seen it over and over again among my former group of friends. When income increases, we immediately upgrade everything to nicer, more expensive versions. We never stop to think, "Do I even like the job that's bringing me all this money?" We just keep doing it, and then we get trapped in that job by all the things we've bought and the loans we took out.

This is particularly true for people who are new to money. Most people spend most of their lives in survival mode, paycheck to paycheck. So why is it, if we're lucky enough to break free from that cycle and be more financially comfortable, the first thing we do is spend more and bring ourselves back to feeling stretched thin, but with nicer things?

It's because our brains are used to the stress of money-worry. And we're creatures of habit, so when something disturbs our pattern of misery, we immediately sabotage it, so we can go back to feeling miserable and complaining about our bad luck.

That's one reason. The other reason is that we're conditioned to compare ourselves to others. Most of us can't help but to look on with a twinge of envy when those around us are doing well. This is especially true when our own success is surpassed by that of someone close to us. It's quite common, and whether you're ready to admit it or not, you've probably experienced this in some way. It might be the thought that immediately precedes your congratulations to the person, and it might be fleeting, but we are inclined to compare ourselves to others in some capacity. I'll admit I used to do this with great regularity.

For me, when the money came, it went just as fast in a public showcase of "look what I can do." It went so fast, in fact, that we became stretched thinner than ever before. This was all put to the test when my dad became ill. He lived with Parkinson's disease for years, which suddenly developed into dementia, and he needed home care. If you've ever had a loved one needing long-term care, you know all too well how expensive it is and how little financial help there is out there. This is oftentimes where inheritances are lost and a reason why generational wealth is so difficult to achieve. Experiencing this has inspired me to teach others about how to acquire and protect generational wealth. I hope to develop this idea someday.

My dad spent his entire life saving his money. He was born in post-World War II Poland and, as an adult, escaped Soviet occupation to come to the United States in the '80s in search of a better life. He achieved it, but he maintained that generationally engrained scarcity mindset that came over with him. He had plenty of money to retire on and a decent sum to pass on to me, his only child, but when he got sick, it all flew out the window in a matter of months. It still makes me sick to think about how he spent his whole life living small when he was at his best, only to spend it all keeping himself alive when he was at his worst.

The funny thing about money, and everything else we desire in life, is that the more we want it, the harder it is to obtain. I'll get into this some more and how to reverse the situation a little bit later in this book. For now, the lesson is that there's so much more to life than money, and when we focus on finding our purpose rather than just chasing money, money naturally follows. We magically have everything we need to live the life we desire, and everything begins to feel easy.

After my dad died, I took some time to reflect. I was neck-deep in my low point during this time and ready to rise again. I didn't know about riding the momentum of change yet, but I knew it was time to do something. The two years preceding my dad's illness showed me I had outgrown my space in Manchester, Connecticut. Getting settled in my thirties, I realized I didn't have as much in common with my friends as I did in my twenties.

When I started Phase 1, I lost my best friends, who were not suited to follow me into my new life. This was a hard pill to swallow, but I later saw why we were meant to part. Toward the end of Phase 1, I lost more friends. Arguing and bickering started showing up in these friendships, seemingly out of nowhere, until there were falling outs that could not and would not be remedied. In my circle of former friends, some chose sides and some chose to remain neutral, but ultimately, it was me who pushed everyone away, even those who stood by me.

I'm not sure exactly what led up to the point of no return with my friends, but it seemed like the change happened over night. An argument came up one day, and it turned the tables. It was a silly argument, but it escalated, and people who were not part of the conversation became involved. I've never had anything like this happen to me before, where something so trivial becomes a relationship-ending catastrophe. It felt like a scene straight out of *Mean Girls*.

I realized, though, that the falling out had nothing to do with the argument. I could feel tension well before this incident happened. Now, with some distance between us and the relationship being mourned and moved on from, I can see things in a better light, and I understand the progression of the conflict.

As I grew and expanded in my mindset and in my businesses, I wanted to be around people who were also growing and expanding. I tried to make my friends rise with me by giving unsolicited advice and pushing them toward doing better. In my perfect world, we all succeeded together and helped one another reach the top.

Reality, however, did not reflect this, and I ended up climbing alone. I got frustrated with my friends when they weren't taking my advice, and they resented me for pushing too hard. A rift was created, although I didn't see it at the time.

I stopped being invited to things, which made me resentful, too. So, we were all just living with resentment toward one another, and I guess that boiled over. We tried to remain cordial with one another, because we had a lot of history. We loosely made up, but there was still tension there. Then, another fight happened over our mutual cleaning lady (this was a *Real Housewives* moment, let me tell you…), and the drama continued.

At some point, I had had enough. I cut off all communication, ignoring flowers sent and condolences expressed after my dad died. I was done and wanted nothing to do with them.

Others in our circle of friends, the neutral parties, were placed at arm's length. Following all the drama, I had trouble trusting anyone who was connected in any way to my former best friends. There was this competition I hadn't signed up for, and I decided to stay away from all of it.

My decision to pull further away from everyone I knew was reinforced after one New Year's Eve experience. We had a small get together at my house, and a friend brought over her boyfriend and a bottle of Veuve. We all settled in to ring in the New Year together. Before the ball dropped, I noticed the couple whispering to each other with their faces glued to their phones. Coincidentally, this was mere minutes after another friend posted a group photo of us on Facebook.

All of a sudden, they had to leave. John had disappeared into the kitchen to throw together his made-from-scratch crab cakes for everyone and didn't even realize what was going on. I don't remember the bullshit excuse they gave, but they grabbed the untapped Veuve that was chilling in the fridge, waiting for midnight, and headed for the door!

John came out of the kitchen and asked what had happened. Dumbfounded, I responded, "I honestly don't know." It was just after 11 p.m., and we were left with half our party, a plate full of crabcakes, and no champagne.

It was pretty obvious that, after that picture was posted, my ex-friends decided to ruin my night. I can only imagine what enticed this couple to leave my house before midnight and go join another party in such a hurry. When I confronted my friend about it later, she put it all on the boyfriend. Tired of the drama, I left it alone and just receded further into my own isolation.

As I recount this, I laugh at how ridiculous it all was, but at the time, it was deeply painful. I was being mean-girled by people whom I wanted nothing to do with. This moment made me lose all faith in anyone who was connected to my former friends. And so, I isolated myself and found peace in my loneliness.

I was alone with my thoughts and had no one to spill them to, except John. Bless his heart, that man wiped so many tears and listened to the same complaints, trying to help me make sense of it all, over and over again. It still doesn't make sense to me, but I've managed to come to terms with it.

In my reflection, I turned to journaling and mindful meditation, which I'd learned during my dad's illness to manage my stress and remain present, so I could make decisions without the cloud of emotions during this difficult time (more on this later). In my journal, I wrote furiously, then angrily, then unhappily, and finally matter-of-factly, where I could analyze objectively what had happened and come to terms with the fact that none of it was my fault. It was therapeutic for me, and I started to piece together where I was and where I wanted to be.

I made a list of things that make me happy and things that make me stressed. I realized that most of the things I was spending my money on did not make the happy list, but money was at the top of my stress list. So, essentially, I was building a cage for myself, creating stress by spending money on things that did not make me happy.

I decided to make a bold move. The money strains of taking care of my dad put us in a hole, so I went to John and said I think we should sell the brand-new GMC Yukon Denali truck we had just bought six months prior, and instead drive the six-year-old Nissan Sentra I'd inherited from my dad.

He was confused, because the Denali was my dream car. He also asked, "How will we fit the kids in the Nissan?" Which was a silly question, because we only had two kids! We had gotten so used to living big, it was hard to imagine fitting a family of four into a regular car with five seatbelts. He also assured me that we would find a way to dig out of the financial hole and could keep the Denali. I insisted we sell it, though.

After we did, I felt so liberated, driving the little beat-up car! I had no one to impress anymore, as all my friends were out of my life, and I had nowhere to go. I also didn't worry about every little ding and scratch like I did with the Denali. I could park it pretty much anywhere, and I blended in everywhere I went.

That last point was an important one for me. I had spent so much time, effort, and money accumulating nice things to impress others. At the time, I would have said, "I'm getting this $100,000 car for me, because I need the space for my family and I like nice things," but as we've already established, that was not true. I wanted to be flashy, I wanted people to be impressed. And that's what I had. I would catch people looking at my car at the gas station, and I got plenty of compliments.

But instead of feeling good about it, I felt threatened. I felt like people wished they could have what I had. Looking back on this now, I'll bet most people didn't give a shit who I was or what I had. They were probably just admiring the car, thinking, "Nice car, but what a waste of money!" I realize now that I was projecting my own insecurities on the situation, because I was always the one wishing I had what others have.

A huge turning point for me was when I was at a gas station with the Nissan, and I realized no one was looking at me and there was a zero percent chance of getting a compliment on my car. I felt so at ease and so happy with my decision to downsize! I also felt much more comfortable with my finances. Just that one change made a huge difference, and John and I felt much better financially.

As I often do, I got carried away by the ease and peace I was feeling at this point in my life. I continued to journal and meditate while I worked out my thoughts and what drove me. I landed on a crazy idea: *Let's just sell everything and start a simpler life in a far, far-away place.*

I brought this fantastic new idea to John, the ever-practical one, who was like, "Huh?" But as can often be seen throughout history, a radical idea starts out as a "no way," then turns into a "that might be kind of cool," then a "maybe," and finally, a "let's do it!"

So, we did. We sold all of our real estate and our house and everything in it. We traded in our two cars for an old Jeep Wrangler. We bought a motorhome, attached the Jeep to the back, loaded it with only the essential things we needed (which was actually a Come-to-Jesus moment, because, when I left our house behind for the auctioneers, it looked like we still lived in it), and we took off on a road trip with our two babies, aged five and two-and-a-half.

We traveled the country for six months, exploring, learning, and getting connected with nature. It was the epitome of stripping down to the essentials and doing some soul-searching. The things we saw and the connections we reestablished within our family were life-altering. We realized how expansive the world really is! Before this, our world had consisted of a twenty-mile radius.

I decided I would spend my time on the road examining myself and figuring out my true purpose. I already had a clear vision of what I didn't want, which was the life I'd left behind. The lack of sadness and remorse I felt when we left was the only confirmation I needed. I knew that, wherever we decided to start over, our lives would be much simpler, with a focus on things that bring us joy.

That place ended up being Spain. In a complicated turn of events that I won't get into here, we decided to try out a new culture, a new climate, and a new pace of life that better aligns with what we value and the type of life we want to create for our family. As I write these words, the transition to my new life is underway, so I have no idea if this is the best idea ever or the worst mistake I've ever made.

One thing I do know is I've become so confident in my ability to thrive that fears no longer hold me back. Despite what happens, I am ready for the next phase, which I plan to share with you in my next book. But for now, let's focus on what led me here.

Through my travels, I did find my purpose, and thus began Phase 2, which consists of implementing my purpose and sharing the process with you by writing this book. The process I took to get here is what this book is about. I kept an inventory of the steps I took and the parts of myself I examined, and I came up with something I call the Purpose Activation Blueprint. And now you can use it, too!

Why Purpose Matters

The word *purpose* seems like a small, abstract, even unimportant word before you begin to dive into the concept and explore the weight behind it. You've probably heard the word a million times and never paid much attention to it. It can mean a variety of things and reference several different subjects.

You can say, "The purpose of a pencil is to write or draw." Or, "The purpose of human life is to survive and reproduce." Here, the word applies to both significant and insignificant subjects, and it can be followed by a wide variety of verbs. The word is so broad, and I think that is why it can be confusing for us to grasp the concept that we all need a purpose in life.

I wish there was a better word in the English language for what I'm talking about here. I am not particularly moved by the word *purpose*. I like to think about the Japanese word *ikigai*, which means a reason for being, a life purpose, or something that makes life worth living. It's a combination of what you love, what you're good at, what the world needs, and what you can be paid for; and teaching you this is exactly the purpose of this book. (See? Even books have purpose!)

Our world is increasingly complex, and it can be difficult to navigate for people who are just existing. We are faced with so many choices, so many opportunities, so many things to fill our time with, and so many places where it could all go wrong.

When we live for a purpose, and not merely "just to exist," we make a commitment to our future selves. We promise we will strive for something that's worth living for, that makes us feel not just alive but full of life. Once we have this commitment in place, the path becomes much more clear. And saying "no" to anything that doesn't suit your purpose becomes easier.

Unfortunately, our society doesn't put much emphasis on the importance of finding one's true purpose. Purpose makes you feel big and impactful. It helps you in decision-making and gives you the confidence to stand up for yourself. You say "no" to things that don't benefit you. Do you know who this purpose-driven person is *not* ideal for? Your boss. It's much more beneficial for corporations to have employees who are just existing, without purpose. I believe this is why finding purpose is not a major focus in our society and definitely not in our education system, where it would change the world.

My issue with society is this: corporations and governments can't control us when we know how to use our intuition, so we've been conditioned to suppress what our bodies tell us. Instead, we listen to the external world to tell us what we need. We blindly follow this trajectory of education, nine-to-five work, babies raised in daycare, pay your taxes, and shut the fuck up. Do you know how revolutionary it would be if everyone on the planet all of a sudden learned to listen to their bodies and acted upon intuitive guidance?

Your body knows what you need. It knows what is best for you. But you've learned to push those urges way down to honor the path that's been laid out for you by the people who seek to profit from the herded-sheep mentality. There's a conspiracy here. It's not a coincidence that schools teach conformity, use standardized testing to assess intelligence despite the evidence that intelligence is multifaceted, and churn out workers instead of thinkers.

I remember, in high school, when I was thinking about what's next, my guidance counselor looked at me confused and asked, "What do you mean 'What's next?' College is next."

I wasn't sure I even wanted to go to college, let alone what I wanted to study. There was never any mention of the other paths to success after high school, like a military career or trade school or entrepreneurship. Some of the kids got the military option, but those of us in honors classes were herded straight to college.

In college, we were instructed to go to career fairs, where the employers were supposed to entice us with six weeks of paid vacation and a few dollars toward retirement and insurance. They tried to make jobs seem scarce, making you think you'd be lucky to work for them.

I know because I was pushed down this conveyor belt. And every time I tried to jump off, there was someone there with a threat or a horror story to set me right back in my place. I rode that conveyor belt right through college, corporate life, graduate school, and academia. When I was in my early thirties, I finally jumped off and refused to get back on.

Although I saw through much of the bullshit while I was in the thick of it, I really began to see the machine that our education system is, when I found myself on the other side of it.

Children are literally taught what to think, what to do, how to behave, what to strive for, and who they are supposed to be from ages five to twenty-five. They come out of the school system different at their core than when they entered. They go in with their true spirit intact and come out conditioned to seek approval, follow the rules, and doubt their own intuition.

I'm not saying that kids should not go to school, and I am 100% not blaming the teachers or administrators (this is a much more global problem). I actually believe children *should* go to school despite its flaws, because the social development that happens while interacting with their peers is incredibly important.

What I am saying, though, is twofold: 1. We must undo the conditioning we have undergone in the education system. (Fortunately, you have embarked on this path just by picking up this book.) And 2. If you have school-aged kids, please keep an eye on what they're saying and how they're changing. You can help them resist the conditioning while it's happening, so they don't need to undo it later on in life. Give them options to express themselves and allow them to discover who they really are, at home and while in your care. Let school be for schooling, but make sure they know they can question what they're learning and not everything out of a textbook is fact.

The big-picture solution would be to overhaul the education system. It needs more flexibility in terms of curriculum diversity rather than a one-size-fits-all approach. We also need more instruction on turning inward and honoring intuition. Kids should be taught to journal their thoughts and reflect on their emotions. They should be encouraged to share their wild theories without judgment. And they should be taught to tolerate others' wild theories.

Self-worth should go beyond grades, allowing kids to detach from external validation. Financial literacy should be taught. Exposure to the various career paths should be introduced early. They should be taught to question everything and engage in critical thinking. I could go on and on.

Unfortunately, for as long as large corporations exist, this will not be possible, because this style of education would produce free thinkers and not employees.

I have good news for you, though. By reading this book and completing the introspective work, you will take the first step toward breaking free from this cycle. You are more of a free thinker than most of the world, because you have chosen to challenge the status quo. You have agreed to explore yourself and ask why you are the way you are. Your boss won't like this, but you are on your way to pursuing a life that fulfills *you*, not one that lines others' pockets.

Do you remember back in the day, when people would "go find themselves" by backpacking through Europe or climbing Mount Everest? We don't hear much about that anymore. Gone are the days of taking time to travel and getting to know ourselves. Understandably so, considering how expensive it is to live, and those who do take a "gap year" often do it for financial reasons without much thought to their existential meaning. College students used to prioritize developing a sense of meaning during this era in their lives, but now the main purpose of college is to provide an entry point into the workforce.

Society has changed, and I think there's a lot to be said for the fact that we live in a world of endless consumerism where everyone seems depressed and anxious and constantly comparing themselves to their peers. This system is designed to keep you broke and unfulfilled, so you will keep working without distraction.

I have a lot of opinions on this subject, but I'll stop here. Suffice it to say, when you find your purpose, you will gain an unshakable confidence that will result in bold moves, displeasing your boss. And *that* is the point of this book.

What to Expect from the Process

Purpose is a fundamental aspect of the human experience. Once we discover our purpose and unapologetically live for it, everything becomes easier. We are better able to make decisions, the actions we need to take become crystal clear, stress is reduced, our important relationships improve, our creativity and productivity shoot through the roof, and our general well-being improves significantly.

That sounds nice, doesn't it? I do have to warn you, though, there are some drawbacks to living your purpose. Once you become fully and absolutely committed to your purpose, some relationships may become strained, much like mine did. I know I said relationship improvement is one of the benefits, but that only refers to the relationships that are meant to continue, the ones that will support you in your new life and make it worth sharing. Some relationships will fall apart when you begin to live at a higher vibration.

The word *relationship* is all-encompassing. I'm referring to friends, family members, coworkers, and even significant others. Here are some descriptions of the relationships you might shed in the process:

> **The you-no-longer-have-things-in-common person:** When you break free from a life of simply existing, you often leave behind habits and vices. There are people with whom you share very little beyond your bad habits and generally negative outlook on life. They're the ones you commiserate with and complain to when life gets overwhelming. They may offer a word of solidarity in the struggle or invite you on a night out for drinks. Although you might feel better immediately after blowing off some steam with them, it doesn't seem like they have much to offer besides company for your misery.

Rising above mere existence will shed light on these people, and you will feel compelled to leave them behind. There will be no hard feelings on your end, but they will no longer serve you in your new life. Usually, these relationships will just fizzle out, and although the other person might feel abandoned, they probably won't hate you.

The jealous-of-your-happiness person: Some people will want to keep you at their level of fulfillment and achievement. When you begin pursuing things that bring you happiness and success, "friends" will crawl out of the woodwork to bring you down. They'll say things like, "you've changed," and "you're not there for me like you used to be." These are people who want something from you. This friendship is for the give-and-take, and usually you're the one giving.

When you begin to focus on things that matter to you and stop catering to their needs, you will see how insignificant these people's problems are, and it will be difficult to dedicate as much time to them as you did before. They will see this as you being a bad friend, and they will give you a hard time. They might even rope others in on this, if there are mutual friendships involved. It will feel like they're ganging up on you, and it will hurt. You will feel betrayed. These friendships end in animosity, and the only way to get through this is to cut these people off completely. (I will share how to do this later in the book.)

The there's-something-about-them-holding-you-back person: These are the relationships that might follow you into your new life at first. The two types of people listed above will fall off quickly, but this person will stick around. They will even console you and support you after the loss of other friends. In general, they are a good friend, but there is something about them that keeps you with one foot still in on your former life.

Maybe this is a coworker from a former job who always talks about work, but you can no longer relate. Or maybe it's a friend of person number 2, who remained neutral in the battle but now transfers energy back and forth between you and your enemy. Either way, this person is not well suited to follow you into your new life. They will always remind you of what you left behind and will stir up negative emotions. You will need to disassociate from this person, consciously and intentionally. This one will be hard, but it's necessary for your growth.

As you can imagine, allowing relationships to fall apart is not easy. This very notion is the reason so many people stay comfortably numb and blissfully ignorant of their life's purpose. Instinctually, we know the process involves the shedding of people and things that no longer serve us, and as creatures of habit, we have a hard time letting go.

You will also lose circumstances that are not meant to come along with you into your new life. When you step fully into living your purpose, things will shift, and your everyday experience will begin to feel different. A job you tolerated might become intolerable; an aggressive client who walks all over you might poke you enough to put them in their place; or being the scapegoat in your family might become a burden you are no longer willing to put up with. You will begin to see your own value, and you will be more willing than ever to stand up for yourself.

This happens because you start to see just *who* you're fighting for—your future self. Becoming that person is so incredibly enticing, you will be willing to let things fall apart just to get a little closer to that version of you. You know that the person you become on the other end of this has your back and the life you're working toward is so deliciously rewarding, you stop caring about the things that stand in your way, even if you cared deeply about them before.

You will also lose habits that no longer suit you. This part took me by surprise, because the things I had an incredibly hard time putting down became revolting to me. I was a major social drinker and pretty much every get-together I had with friends involved cocktails at a bar or wine at home. But when I started on my purpose journey, I was finding, whenever I drank alcohol, even a little bit, I didn't feel like my best self. And I had big things to accomplish—enjoying my RV trip to the fullest, starting my new business, writing the book you're holding in your hands—so every time I was not at my best, I felt trapped and stagnant.

I tried to cut back and keep my drinking just to the weekends, but no matter how hard I tried to change the pattern, I still found I was disgusted with myself the morning after. I also didn't like the idea of my kids growing up, seeing a drink in my hand almost every night. I don't want them to think that drinking at the end of the day is the only way to wind down and relax, nor do I want them to remember me as an altered version of myself.

So, I did the thing I thought I would never be able to do. I stopped drinking. Fully stopped. I told myself I was going to be sober for six months, while I went through the process of finishing this book and releasing it into the world. While I'm still in that six-month range as I write these words, I can't see myself ever going back to the way I was. I'm not saying I'll never drink again, but I've become so addicted to the sober version of myself, I can't imagine giving up this feeling.

Other habits melted away, and new, productive ones popped up, too. I stopped watching TV in the evening after the kids went to bed and started reading. I got my family to do chores each day, so the house would stay tidy and we didn't need to do a big clean every couple of weeks. We started cooking meals at home (and by *we*, I mean John, because he's the chef around here). I used to *love* eating out, but all of a sudden, it felt less fun, and I preferred a healthy, balanced meal at home.

It might be hard to imagine the same changes I've been talking about coming to life for you. I felt that way, too. Our habits infuse our lives from every angle, and they determine who we are and how we feel about ourselves. It might feel like you're standing in front of a mountain and I'm asking you to get your shit together and climb it, but I promise you, it's not actually very hard. It kind of happens naturally, once you start moving toward your purpose. Your body tells you what to shed.

You go through a molting process, where you leave behind your old skin and grow into a new, more comfortable, better-suited one. This can be painful. There is a sense of loss and oftentimes a grieving process that follows, but once that is done, the pure peace that comes with living your life's purpose makes it all worthwhile.

The Purpose Activation Blueprint Approach

When I set out to find my purpose, it was done with absolute intention. I didn't stumble upon this idea, nor did it happen by chance. For some people, though, it does happen that way. By gravitating naturally toward various opportunities in life, they may find the thing they were meant to do. Those people are lucky enough to flow into their purpose, and their lives seem naturally easy. For some, this happens relatively early in life, and they get to spend their entire existence on Earth in an aligned and easeful flow.

Others stumble upon their purpose later in life. This is more common, because it's after they've had a chance to try on many hats. Most people, however, never find their purpose, and they spend their entire lives just getting by. The good news, though, is even if you haven't been lucky enough to stumble into your purpose, the very fact that you're reading this book means you have a good chance of finding it intentionally. Awareness is eighty percent of the work, and going through this process will bring you more in alignment with your true purpose and happiness.

In my studies of manifestation and the Law of Attraction earlier on in my life, I learned about purpose, so, I knew the importance of finding it in order to live a fulfilling life. When my world came crashing down around me and the life I thought I had built around my purpose turned out to be superficial, I knew I had work to do.

It all started with journaling. I started to write aimlessly, and then I became more focused and intentional. I gave myself prompts, wrote at specific times in a specific way, and analyzed the results. I found that there were seven key elements that emerged to describe my purpose. Later, I explored these principles further by working with various people on finding their purpose in life, and what I found was that every purpose can be broken down into these seven elements.

I felt like I had found the answer to human existence! My methods were reproducible, and I knew I could help others. So, in alignment with my own purpose, I set out to help others find theirs.

I was blown away by the feedback I got and the clientele I was attracting! I had several very successful people knock at my door, wanting to be coached by me. I will introduce you to some of them in a bit. They went on to absolutely flip their lives upside down in order to live their purpose, and they grew to be happier than ever before.

I, then, decided to isolate the Purpose Activation Blueprint from my coaching work, so it could be more accessible and available to more people without a high coaching price tag. I wrote out the steps I was teaching and the journal prompts I refined and then decided to write the very book you're holding in your hands. This book will guide you through the theory behind the system and will show you how to analyze your own responses, so you can come to your own conclusions. Although I can't lay out every single path you are meant to take as an individual in this format, like I would with my coaching students, I can provide some general guidance to steer you toward a life that will bring you happiness and joy.

Eventually, I'd like to adapt the Purpose Activation Blueprint into a self-paced course, so it can reach more people without the restriction of how much I can physically handle as one human being. I believe this system will change countless lives, and I want it in the hands of as many people as possible. Stay tuned to my social media for the progress on that!

The next several chapters will cover the principles behind the key elements to purpose. Each chapter will also contain various suggestions for opening up the flow of consciousness, and journal prompts that are associated with each element. Once all seven elements are explored thoroughly, I will walk you through the analysis process and provide some advice on what to do next.

Be forewarned, though: in this format, I cannot analyze every aspect of your responses. I also can't give you individualized advice for how to get from point A to point B, like I would in my coaching program. What I can provide is a starting point. I will help you come to a conclusion about what your purpose in life is, based on several factors contained within your journal responses.

With that being said, I invite you to keep reading. I may be biased, but I think the ideas contained here are eye opening and tap into your intuition to guide you in an innovative way. If nothing else, I can guarantee you will have a new approach to analyzing your happiness and considering facets of yourself you may not have thought of before when making big decisions.

CHAPTER 1

The Foundations of Purpose

THERE ARE SEVERAL WAYS to find happiness in life. New love sparks passion. Achieving a big goal makes us feel on top of the world. And bringing in lots of money makes us feel accomplished. Notice any commonalities among these three bringers of happiness? They are all temporary! Love can last, but it doesn't stay new and exciting forever. Reaching a goal feels pretty good, but that feeling dissipates, especially if the momentum stops. I think we all know the story with money. Yes, it might bring a jolt of happiness, but it cannot sustain it.

True and lasting happiness comes from a less exciting place. It comes from within, and it requires a slow and steady stream of fulfillment and satisfaction. Any of the factors above can be ripped away in an instant, so they are not good examples of long-term happiness.

The 2023 Ipsos Global Happiness Study and other research has found that there are three important things that bring consistent, predictable happiness. Don't get too excited, because they are pretty dull. But that, in essence, is what makes them consistent and predictable, and that's why they can sustain long-term happiness, while other things bring only fleeting happiness. The following factors have been found to be strong predictors of happiness:

Strong relationships. The Harvard Study of Adult Development followed participants for over eighty years. It was found that strong and supportive relationships are one of the most consistent predictors of happiness and health. This does not necessarily equate to a romantic relationship, though. People who have strong social networks and supportive friendships can be just as happy as those who have a significant other.

It's also important to note here that having a significant other does not always mean that the relationship is a supportive one. Companionship does not automatically combat loneliness, and people who stay in toxic relationships tend not to be happy. The strong relationships the study references are those that provide deep connection, emotional safety, and mutual growth over time.

Good Physical and Mental Health. There have been tons of studies that support the idea that physical activity is associated with lower rates of depression and better mood. Better mood is generally linked with higher levels of resiliency and a positive life outlook.

Financial Stability. Didn't I just say that money can't sustain happiness? I did, and there's a difference between stability and wealth. A 2010 study suggests that income affects emotional well-being, but only up to a certain threshold. That threshold was $75,000 at the time (just over $100,000 in 2025, adjusted for inflation). This means that people's happiness is only affected by money to the extent of attaining stability and safety. Money itself is not what brings happiness. It's what it can provide for us that matters.

The nice thing about these factors is they are all relatively within our control. It's not like I'm saying you have to be born to a billionaire or be the most attractive person within a fifty-mile radius. Those things are beyond your control and, coincidentally, fall pretty low on the list of things that make us consistently and predictably happy.

For the most part, you can make changes in your lifestyle if you're lacking in any of these three areas. You can change your mindset, better your health, control who gets to share in your energy, and change your financial situation. Making these changes requires real work, but it's 100% possible, and following the principles in this book will help to steer you in the right direction.

Common Misconceptions

As we've established, *purpose* is a confusing word. Amidst the confusion and general disregard for its importance in our society, many people don't quite understand it. It's not your fault, though. The steps for finding purpose, in my opinion, are something that should be taught in schools. We should be talking about this, starting in first grade, and there should be courses on it in college. But don't forget, schools are part of the system, and the system's job is to churn out worker bees.

In an effort to make it more clear and to perfectly define the idea of a life's purpose, let's debunk some misconceptions. Here are some common ideas people tend to have about purpose and why they're not true:

Purpose is all about career: We often think of purpose in the context of what we do for work. This makes sense because we spend at least thirty-three percent of each weekday committed to work. In reality, though, purpose can be derived from other sources. It can come from a hobby, parenthood, philanthropy, and many others!

Purpose is linear: We are not born with a singular, unchanging path to purpose. Personality loosely aligns with purpose, and some aspects of personality are innate, but our path changes as we grow and experience the world. Purpose also shifts as we enter different eras in our lives. (More on this later.)

Purpose guarantees happiness: Finding your purpose and living by it makes decision-making easier. At a core level, you might feel aligned, like you're exactly where you need to be, but this does not equal happiness. In fact, in the beginning, things become harder for a while. When you set out to fulfill your purpose, it requires work to put the pieces of your new life into place.

Disappointments are bound to happen. The process requires sacrifice and the shedding of things and relationships that no longer serve you. Life can actually feel quite lonely for some time. But once you get settled into your life's purpose, happiness and peace often follow the heartache.

As you can see, there are a lot of facets to the idea of a life's purpose. Before I started my work and research, I believed all of the above to be true. I floundered in the idea that finding purpose is this soul-enlightening, grand journey to nirvana, full of trippy epiphanies and metaphors and symbols. In reality, the journey looks a whole lot like a typical Tuesday. You just go about your life, making small changes in your thoughts and actions until you have a better understanding of what fills your cup. It requires bold moves, but there's no reason those moves can't be calculated and well-prepared.

One of the steps toward my life's purpose involved living in an RV with my family for six months. I sold almost everything I owned and crammed my family into a forty-foot motorhome to drive around the country. It took me a year to prepare for this bold move, and trust me, there were doubts. I needed to do a ton of planning, and it required a whole lot of trust in the process. The good news, though, is that, when you're on the right path, there are encouraging signs that will let you know you're doing the right thing. I'll clue you in on what to look out for in Chapter 10.

Beginning Your Purpose Activation Blueprint

The next several chapters contain the instructions for completing your Purpose Activation Blueprint. We've done the concept work, and hopefully your juices are flowing with ideas of what fulfills you and brings you joy. Soon, we will take those ideas and shape them into structured, calculated concepts to use as building blocks for uncovering your life's purpose.

I want you to take your time with this process. In my coaching, the entire Purpose Activation Blueprint takes six months to construct, from conceptualization to finished product. A lot of internal work goes into this, and sometimes the answers you need are buried deep within you. You might take this a bit faster than I do in coaching, but I suggest you work on your blueprint for at least seven weeks, which boils down to one chapter per week.

Please take each section and each reflective activity slowly. Sit with your responses for a couple of days before moving on. You might notice that thoughts come to you like rapid fire while you're journaling, but those are only from the surface level and may just be a reflection of whomever society has conditioned you to become. They might not be your true, unfiltered feelings. When you sit with your responses for a few days and fleetingly think about them throughout the day, you might stumble upon some important ideas.

This happens because, while your brain is distracted doing other things, your true, uninhibited thoughts surface, even if it's just for a moment. Not to dive too deep into Freudian psychology, but your brain has a gatekeeper called the Ego. This gatekeeper keeps you in your proper place in the world. It operates by the principles of its counterpart, the Superego. As it's filtering your thoughts, the Ego considers social norms and limits you to where society has determined you belong. It's the little voice that says, "That dream is too big, it'll never happen for someone like you." This is its way of suppressing the thoughts of the Id, the Ego's other counterpart, which operates on primal thoughts and desires and disregards social expectations. The Id is what we want to tap into during your Purpose Activation Blueprint work.

There's no way to turn off the Ego, but there are ways to distract it. In your sleep, for example, the Ego drifts off, and you might experience your uninhibited thoughts. You might wake up and think, *What the heck did I just dream?* That was just your Id, being its primal, unfiltered self. That's actually a glimpse into the real you! Also, when you're engrossed in your daily activities, your filter can be turned off, because your Ego is busy keeping you from embarrassing yourself.

This is why it's important to spend some time writing each day and dedicate several days to each section before moving on. Your Ego might let some thoughts slip during your sleep or daily activities. You won't notice it when it happens, but when you sit down to complete your journaling, the thought might resurface because it was active not too long ago.

Another recommendation for working through the Purpose Activation Blueprint is to dedicate time to it. Block off at least thirty minutes each day or every other day for at least seven weeks to ensure you have plenty of time for reflection. The best time of day for reflection is either first thing in the morning or right before you go to bed at night.

I journal during both times of day for different reasons. I do some journaling before bed, so the ideas I'm working on are front and center when I fall asleep. It brings me some creativity when the Ego is resting. Then, when I wake up, I do some writing to capture that creativity on paper. You do what works best for you and your schedule, but please do schedule the time with yourself. Put it in your calendar, set reminders on your phone, or do whatever you need to do to ensure you will show up for yourself.

I also suggest writing your responses out on paper, rather than typing them on a computer or on your phone. There are several reasons for this. There is magic in putting pen to paper, because it strengthens the neural pathways you're developing. But more logistically-speaking, we will be analyzing your responses later on in the process. This will require highlighting and/or underlining specific words and phrases to identify themes and sentiments within your responses. This is best done on paper.

You can use any blank notebook or you can purchase the companion workbook for this book, called *The Purpose Activation Blueprint Workbook*. My workbook contains all of the prompts you'll find in this book organized by chapter with some space for your written responses. The final analysis for completing your Purpose Activation Blueprint is outlined for you in the workbook, as well, making it easy to use as a complement to your reading journey. I've also included some bonus prompts for deeper reflective work.

And finally, please track which chapter contains each reflection and the title of the prompt. In our analysis, you will need to refer to specific responses, so this will make it easier to locate what you need.

And now, ladies and gentlemen, without further ado, let's get started.

CHAPTER 2

The Power of Self-Awareness

PURPOSE IS A UNIQUE concept for every individual. It's kind of like a fingerprint. It may look similar to others', with the swirls and the lines, but when you analyze it deeply, you will see that everyone has a unique one. So reliably unique, in fact, that we can confidently identify a person based on their fingerprint. Similarly, we can analyze a person based on their purpose.

One of the most critical determining factors in purpose is one's own beliefs. It's important to consider what you believe about the world, but even more vital is what you believe about yourself—your abilities, your strengths, your flaws, etc. This analysis can become problematic because so many facets of ourselves are clouded by social conditioning. We take on and internalize deeply what others say to us, the feedback we get from the world, and what we say to ourselves.

I had an English teacher tell me in my senior year of high school that my writing is "subpar and superficial." This was on a paper I was extremely proud of and thought I was going to ace. English was my favorite subject, and in the previous year, I'd had the most inspiring, thought-provoking teacher who'd given me awesome feedback. I felt confident in my writing until I met this guy, whose comment brought me to tears. I started to doubt myself and began to hate creative writing. I avoided it at all costs, until I started writing this very book. I'm thirty-five right now, so imagine—this one dude's very subjective opinion of me shaped my reality for *seventeen years*.

I've finally been able to push past this judgment because of the introspective work I've done recently. I reconnected with the fact that I love writing and love expressing myself genuinely. I've done the exercises I'm going to have you do, and when I looked back on my childhood to consider what I loved doing, I realized I used to keep journals. As a kid, I used to write every night and express my desires, my thoughts, and my dreams. I also realized I stopped keeping those journals right around the time I went to college. Is it a coincidence that I stopped this habit right after my writing was criticized? I think not.

So, I went back to journaling. And the floodgates opened on my creativity. This very book poured out of me so fast, I had to outline the sections and quickly write cryptic notes for myself so I wouldn't miss an idea.

I've come across tons of examples like this in my own introspection. For some of them, I had to dig deep to challenge my core belief because, if the situation that shaped it happened today, it wouldn't have affected me. But this is the problem—we tend to analyze things from our current perspective. My thirty-five-year-old self would have told Mr. W to kick rocks (I hope he reads this!), but my eighteen-year-old self was deeply affected.

We have to delve into our past and approach a belief from the perspective of our childhood selves to really analyze how it formed and why. When you come across a core belief that you're not sure is your own, try to trace it back to where it came from, but from your younger self's perspective.

Introspection

In the Purpose Activation Blueprint, we examine the many facets of an individual, which begins with *introspection*, or the act of deep self-reflection. We start by evaluating self-concept, which is broken down into two pieces: core beliefs and values. We will look at core beliefs in this chapter and values in the next.

Exploring your self-concept, or how you view yourself, can be a transformative journey. Even though we live with ourselves every day, most of us don't think about why we are the way we are. You might be able to describe yourself in five words, but what if I asked you to tell me why you are those things?

When you really boil it down, most of your character is shaped by society. Beneath that layer of social conditioning is where your true character can be found. Often, it is suppressed or changed entirely by the feedback you've gotten from the world. Beneath my avoidance of writing was a kid who actually loved writing and found it to be a form of therapeutic self-expression. This is my true character, and I'm beyond thrilled to have reconnected with this part of myself.

Later in this chapter, I outline some tasks that will help you examine your self-concept and how it was shaped through your core beliefs. You can do these as many times as you'd like, until you feel sure you've captured all the thoughts and ideas buried deep beneath the socially conditioned surface of your being.

Your mission for this section is to get to know yourself at an uninhibited level. I want you to reconnect with the childhood you, before expectations, pressures, and norms got ahold of you. When you really and truly know yourself, you become unshakable in your confidence. You will know your weaknesses and your actual limitations, not the ones society says you have. This is fundamental for understanding your true self-concept.

Identifying Your Core Beliefs

Your belief system was constructed a long time ago. Sometimes unknowingly, we hold onto the beliefs we developed as children. Someone important in your life may have made a comment that you've never forgotten or you witnessed a pattern of behavior in someone you looked up to, so now, that core belief has shaped the foundation for how you see yourself and the world. This is largely unconscious, taking shape behind the scenes, but it's often irrational and not based in facts. These beliefs determine how we see the world and, as a result, how it treats us.

Psychology named this *confirmation bias*, which means we look for confirmation from our environment that our beliefs are true and correct, while ignoring anything to the contrary. Let me give you an example. If a child believes they are fundamentally bad at math, they will look for clues to support this belief. They might focus on the problems they got wrong, assuming their mistakes are just more confirmation that they are bad at math. When they get problems right, they might downplay the success, thinking the problems were easy or they just got lucky.

Confirmation biases reflect our thoughts and how we believe things work in the world. Often, these beliefs lead to actions, which results in what's called a *self-fulfilling prophecy*. The kid who is bad at math might put less effort into studying and avoid activities that involve math, because they think, *What's the use?* This leads to poor performance on tests and homework assignments, reinforcing the belief that they are just simply bad at math.

Can you think of an example in your life where you have a confirmation bias? I'm sure you have plenty. We all do. It's just hard to pinpoint, because these aren't just thoughts we can interrupt and change. These are fundamental beliefs about who we are.

So where do these beliefs come from? Why are we so hard on ourselves, believing the worst about our abilities? It's because we're almost *too* conscious. We're the most evolved animal on the planet, able to think and plan and analyze, but there's a problem. Thinking is subjective, not factual. The way I think is different from the way you think. I approach problems and tasks from my level of understanding and how I perceive the world, and you approach from yours. Neither of us is right or wrong. We just think differently, and we have different belief systems in place from which our analysis of the world originates.

The core of the problem is that beliefs do not equal facts, because everything in our reality is based on perception. I happen to think I'm quite intelligent, but there are people out there who are a hell of a lot smarter than I am, and they probably think I'm pretty average. Even the metrics that attempt to define things like intelligence have flaws. An IQ test can put a number on my intelligence, but it cannot factor in every possible facet of human cognition. So, even when the information that shapes our beliefs comes from a scientific, fact-based source, it often fails to paint an accurate picture of the whole situation.

Our system of beliefs is implemented starting at a young age. Our parents and teachers have *a lot* of influence on who we become as adults. A child's mind is extremely receptive to feedback because they are still working out their self-concept. So, when a teacher, who is an authority figure on all things related to intelligence from a child's perspective, casually says to a kid, "Math is not your strongest subject," the kid takes it to heart and generates a core belief.

It's not just words that help shape our core beliefs. We also absorb others' actions and beliefs. For example, a child grows up watching their parents work long hours and emphasize the importance of hard work and perseverance. They see their parents getting promotions and recognition for their hard work. This child internalizes the idea that hard work leads to success and the self-fulfilling prophecy begins to take shape.

They work hard at school, get good grades, and try to be the best in everything they do. They get praise from their parents and teachers for their results. They've just proven to themselves that hard work does, in fact, lead to success, thus strengthening their confirmation bias. This child may grow up to be surprised that they are not great at everything, no matter how hard they work. They may also be frustrated to see others finding success with minimal effort doing aligned work, while they slave away trying to work their way up.

A lot of who we are is, fortunately or unfortunately, shaped by the actions and beliefs of our parents. There is good news, though. Once you identify your limiting core beliefs, the ones that hold you back from reaching your full potential, you can undo them. The activities I have outlined for you in the next section will help you sort through your core beliefs and eliminate the ones that do not serve you.

Chapter 2 Exploration Exercises

Following are the activities to help you map out your self-concept. Please take your time with these. Introspection is a slow process because you have to navigate around your Ego. I suggest you spend a week on these activities, returning to them multiple times.

1. **Reflecting on Limiting Beliefs**

This exercise is meant to reveal your limiting beliefs and reconnect you with the forgotten version of yourself. With everything you just learned about core beliefs in mind, spend some time answering the following questions:

- What do I believe about myself that holds me back? Where do these beliefs come from?
- What fears do I have about failure?
- What fears do I have about success? (Yes, there are always fears associated with success!)
- When have I felt unworthy or undeserving, and why?
- What sparked joy in me as a child?
- What were some of the things I liked to do as a child?
- What did I pretend to be when playing make-believe in my childhood?
- What was my favorite subject in school? Not strongest subject. *Favorite* subject.

2. Challenging Core Beliefs

List a few core beliefs you hold about yourself (e.g., "I'm not creative" or "I don't deserve success"). For each belief, ask yourself:

- Is this belief absolutely true?
- What evidence do I have to support this belief?
- What evidence contradicts this belief?
- How would my life change if I didn't hold this belief?

3. Ideal Self Visualization

Visualization helps you acknowledge the gap between your current self-concept and the person you aspire to be. It also highlights limiting beliefs that are preventing you from achieving this ideal version.

- Right before you fall asleep at night, visualize an ideal version of yourself who has overcome limiting beliefs and reached goals. Envision what this New You is wearing, how they look, what they're doing, etc. Be as specific as possible in your visualization.
- When you wake up in the morning, journal your thoughts. Free write for a few minutes, and then list the differences between your ideal self and your current self.

CHAPTER 3

Uncovering Your Authentic Values

ANOTHER ASPECT OF THE self-concept is what you value. While core beliefs shape your views at a fundamental but largely unconscious level, values directly impact your identity. They're a little more obvious than core beliefs, and we can often see them in other people through their behaviors and words. We often label people based on their values (e.g., based on religion, political views, their interpretation of right and wrong, etc.). One problem, though, is that society and our environment teach us what to value in many respects, so we often walk through life valuing things that don't actually resonate with us on a deep level.

The goal in this chapter is to comb through your set of values and identify which ones are true to your being and which ones have been instilled in you. It is critical to note here that some values society has us buy into are not terrible. For example, it's socially normal to value law and order and respect for authority. I don't think it's a good idea to reprogram those values. But things like conformity (fitting in) and material wealth are values we could do without.

What Values Mean

Values are important because they guide your decision-making and give you a sense of pride or failure based on who you are and what you accomplish. When we honor our values, we feel aligned and proud of ourselves. When we dishonor them, we feel something called *cognitive dissonance*, which is a mental tension that occurs when our actions do not match our values or beliefs. I'm sure you've experienced cognitive dissonance before.

For example, you might value honesty, but one day, you tell a lie for whatever reason. This action dishonors your value and creates immense discomfort in your mind. The more you value honesty, the more this will bother you. This is how you determine the strength of your value—the more uncomfortable you are after dishonoring it, the more important it is to you. To alleviate the discomfort, you have two choices: you can try to justify the action so it fits into your belief system, or you can change the action.

After your lie is told, you might say to yourself, "I said that for a good reason." If you truly value honesty, you're probably not someone who lies lightly just for fun, so this rationale might suffice. If the action continues to eat away at you, you might come clean and tell the person the truth. This will definitely get rid of the cognitive dissonance, because now your action matches your value.

Evaluating your values system and assessing whether or not you're living your life based on your true standards can be a complicated process. Unfortunately, society has trained us to behave a certain way, so, even if those behaviors don't align with our true values, we think they're okay because we operate on this deep, incorrect programming that has been installed in our minds.

This is an incorrect assumption. You are not required to comply with society's standards in any way. There is no correct path for a successful life. So often, we (myself included) get so carried away with what success is supposed to look like, we don't stop to think if the "success" we're after actually makes us feel happy and aligned.

The Origin of Values

A truly integral part of introspection is filtering out the values and beliefs that did not originate from within you. In the last chapter, we worked on beliefs established in your mind by others. Now, it's time to examine the values society has deemed you are responsible for. We'll also take it a step further and look at how society cons you into justifying the behaviors they want you to engage in, even when they don't align with your values.

Values come from lots of different origins. Some we adopt from our parents, others we come up with ourselves (sometimes despite our parents), and still others are activated in us by society. This is all okay, as long as all of these values serve a purpose and actually make us feel fulfilled.

It's when our values create struggle or conflict that's a problem. This can happen for many reasons. As we grow, our needs evolve and our place in the world shifts. Naturally, our values shift as well, but not without a fight.

The process begins slowly, with subtle doubts cast upon our old values system. Back when I was teaching and advising students, I had a student named Mel, who went through this molting process in her political views. Mel was raised in a political household, where her father served as an alderman for the town. I won't say in which direction, but her family strongly aligned with one side of the political aisle. They spoke harshly about the other side in their home and mocked supporters of their political opponents.

When Mel went to college, away from these discussions at the dinner table, she began exploring her political values. She met new people from different backgrounds and heard new perspectives. At first, Mel had a hard time listening to those people's stories, often chalking their experiences up to a fundamental problem with the person, not the system. But as time went on, she heard similar stories from different people and started to wonder if it was not, in fact, the system that was failing, rather than the people. This was the opposite of what she was taught, growing up.

When Mel came to me for academic advising, our work ended up going beyond just picking classes. We started meeting twice a week to continue the conversation about how she was struggling with her identity (these were her words, not mine). She described the person she thought she was, but she did so with contempt in her voice.

When she was finished, I asked simply, "Do you like the person you just described?"

Without hesitation, she let out a heavy and emotional, "No."

This realization set the tone for the remainder of our conversations. I worked with Mel on reworking her self-concept to better match her evolving values. There were a lot of steps, and some of them involved having difficult conversations with her family. At the end of our work together, though, Mel felt more aligned with her true self and her purpose.

This one shift in identity led Mel to new opportunities that were better aligned with the person she was becoming. At first, she painted a picture for me of what she expected her life would look like, with the dreary, boring, run-of-the-mill career her parents expected her to fall into and a life she thought was inevitable but was not looking forward to. When we were finished, she pivoted in her studies and went in an entirely different direction. As far as I know, Mel continues to live her purpose and works in a field that lights up her soul and gives her life meaning. She makes way less money than her parents expected her to, but money is not a core value of Mel's, so she's happy.

I hope that something about Mel's story has resonated with you. This example can be adapted to many different values that we've absorbed from our parents. From religion to views on wealth and money, our parents had opinions when we were growing up, and to some extent, those opinions shaped our values. The pivotal point to remember, though, is that these are not the values we were meant to die with. We can change.

I'll give you one more quick example from my own life. This one involves societal conditioning and the value we are taught to place on material possessions and external indicators of success. When I was in my late twenties and early thirties, I started making much more money as my business and my real estate portfolio took off. But the more money I made, the more money I spent. Looking back, it all happened so fast, I don't even know what the hell I was thinking. Before I knew it, I had multiple Louis Vuittons, $150,000-worth of cars (and an equivalent amount of debt), and a new hot tub. All totally unnecessary and extravagant.

When I looked around, I barely recognized my life. I came from a frugal upbringing and had always been the one who had less than everyone else. My friends' parents didn't allow them to come over to my house because I lived in a "dangerous neighborhood." I was the kid whom my friends' parents felt bad for. So, my new showcase of prosperity was foreign to me, and it didn't feel as good as I thought it would.

When I evaluated my behaviors, I realized I was operating from values originating outside of myself. Society puts a lot of emphasis on appearance and material possessions. We're always looking at what others have and wishing we had it, too. I'll admit, when I had the means to, I rushed to keep up with the Joneses.

I decided I didn't like myself that way. I didn't like seeing the money flowing out of my bank account faster than it was coming in. I didn't like the astronomical loan balance I saw when I pulled my credit report. And I didn't like how I worried about protecting it all.

When I decided to sell it all, it was like a weight had been lifted. It started with my beautiful Denali. It wasn't just the money I was saving by not paying that ridiculous loan payment; it was also the relief from worrying about parking far away from the store to avoid dings and scratches and skipping parallel parking because I might (and did) scratch the rims.

When I sold that SUV and felt the wave of relief rush over me, I realized that the significance I placed on material possessions was not true to my core values. When actions align with values, harmony exists. But for me, there was dissonance. I wondered what else in my set of values came from external sources.

The last thing to go was my beloved house. It was just over 2,000 beautiful square feet of hard work and meticulous renovations and decorating we had done, when we bought it four years prior. We put a lot of money and effort into that house. We worked hard to make it a home for our little family. My daughter was almost one when we bought it and my son was born while we lived there. It was the only house they knew, and we had a lot of great memories there.

They each had their own room, and they shared a bathroom, but what I noticed was how they much preferred to sleep close to us, and everyone brushed their teeth in the master bathroom. We had a formal living room and a dining room, but no one was allowed to hang out in there. We called it "the other side," and the furniture was too expensive to actually enjoy with kids around. My office was in the finished basement, where I spent entirely too much time with no access to natural light. Ironically, in order to pay for all this unused but beautiful space, I had to spend most of my day in the dreariest part of the house.

I realized that more than half of the house was wasted space. John and I always wanted to be near each other when we weren't working, and our kids wanted to be on top of us every moment of every day, so we were always contained within the same 200 square feet anyway.

So, we sold that, too. We bought a forty-foot motorhome and decided to take some time exploring this beautiful country of ours. Then, we planned to hop on a plane and move to Spain. Now, *that* decision created harmony within me. It was sad leaving our beloved house, but the joy of living on our terms and unloading the baggage weighing us down was worth the sadness a million times over.

This is an example of how society cons us into pursuing things that don't align with our true values. We are shown images of what "success" looks like, and it always involves nice houses and cars, designer clothing, and an expensive lifestyle. What society doesn't show us is that the best indicator of success is freedom. Freedom of time to do what we enjoy, freedom of choosing our environment, and freedom of spending money on things that actually bring us joy are what really matter.

It took me thirty-something years to clear the bullshit from my life and begin living a life that's true to my values. I didn't even know I was striving toward goals that weren't mine until I reached them! You probably are, too.

Chapter 3 Exploration Exercises

These exercises are meant to help you identify your values and separate them from the values you've adopted from external sources. Again, please take your time with these and return to the activities a few times over the course of the next week.

1. **Values List**

Separate your genuine internal values from those installed in you by focusing on what truly resonates with you. List twenty values (e.g., honesty, success, family, freedom) on a piece of paper. Rank them in order of personal importance. For each value, ask:

- Why is this important to me?
- Would this value still matter if no one else knew about it?

2. **The Five Whys**

Uncover the root motivations behind your values. Choose your top five values from your Values List (e.g., financial success) and ask yourself "Why?" five times, each time digging deeper into the reason behind that value. For example:

Q: Why is financial success important to me?

A: Because I want to feel secure.

Q: Why do I want security?

A: Because security makes me feel stable.

Q: Why do I feel insecure without financial stability?

A: Because I fear what will happen if I can't pay my mortgage.

Q: What will happen if I can't pay for my mortgage?

A: We will need to downsize our house and sell our things.

Q. What does it mean if we have to downsize?

A: It means I have failed my family.

In this example, the core value is driven by the desire to provide stability for family. If the last question was answered, "People will judge us," the value is driven by appearances and social perception. The goal here is to get to the bottom of what you value and to examine whether your driving factors really are motivating to you when stripped down to basic desires.

3. The Should vs. Want Exercise

Identify where outside sources might be influencing your choices and values.

- Create two columns: "What I should do" (according to society, family, or culture) and "What I want to do." Write down actions, goals, and values that fall into each category.

- If any of your items falls under both columns, do some real thinking about whether those desires truly resonate with you or if they're just so deeply ingrained, you believe them to be yours when they're actually an expectation set up for you.

  It might be helpful to do the Five Whys exercise from #2 on the ones that fall under both columns.

CHAPTER 4

Tapping into Your Unique Talents and Strengths

EVERYONE HAS UNIQUE talents and strengths that shape their identity and sense of purpose. Usually, being good at something allows us to enjoy it more because it can be done with ease. We tend to excel at some things, and others we have to work at. This is the fundamental difference between talents and strengths. Talents are our natural abilities, and strengths are abilities that we develop over time with practice.

Talents are expressed naturally. They can be things like musical, artistic, or athletic ability, problem-solving, leadership, nurturing, and empathy, among others. A talent is something you have a "knack" for and was probably recognized at a young age. It's something that comes easily to you, while others have a hard time picking it up.

It's important to note, however, that talents may sometimes go unnoticed when the environment is not conducive to fostering the talent. For example, if a child is naturally athletic but is never enrolled in any sports programs or given the chance to practice their athleticism, they probably won't reach their fullest potential. Even though they come naturally, talents require nurturing in order to be fully realized.

Strengths, on the other hand, are built over time. They're developed through experiences, learning, and consistent effort. They fill in the spaces where natural talents don't quite exist, but you have to be willing to put in the effort to develop the skill. We've all seen this when we were school-aged children. One student gets As without much effort, while another gets As because they bust their butt studying and learning.

Examining your strengths and talents is an integral part of finding your place in the world. Understanding what you can contribute by tapping into what's already inside of you helps to align you with your purpose.

Leveraging Strengths in Your Purpose

Your purpose lies at the intersection of what you're good at, what you enjoy, and what the world needs. Seems simple enough, right? We have to be good at whatever we're dedicating our lives to, otherwise we won't excel. And if we don't excel, we're less likely to enjoy the experience. Now, it's certainly possible to practice your way to greatness, but there must be some fundamental level of talent and ability that underlies the effort.

Take for example an Olympic figure skater. Figure skaters aren't born with a pair of ice skates on their feet (although some seem like they were). Their accomplishments are a result of ability, talent, and perseverance. First comes ability. When a figure skater is born, they are not able to hit the ice immediately. They need to develop the strength in their legs to hold them up.

Once they can walk, they are often brought straight to the ice rink by parents with high hopes. Then, their natural talents are put to the test. Some kids will take to the sport immediately, spinning and twirling by their third birthday, while others will need more time and practice. Both types of young skaters, at this point, could have a shot at the Olympics. Some kids need more time to develop physically, but it doesn't mean they will be behind forever.

After training for a decade, however, the ones who have significantly fallen behind their Olympic-bound peers might be coming to the realization that their talent is not good enough for their dream. More than likely, though, this realization comes with a mixture of sadness and relief, because they probably stopped enjoying their sport a while ago.

When we're not good at something, we tend not to get as much satisfaction from it as we do from things we are good at. Let me be clear here. I'm not talking about leisure activities. I'm talking about life-purpose activities. You can be a terrible painter and enjoy the shit out of painting landscapes that you know aren't great, but you hang them up in your house anyway. That's fantastic! But chances are you will not fulfill your life's purpose as an artist who sells their paintings to others. I will get more into this later, but your purpose requires some level of service to others, and your landscapes probably don't spark as much joy in others as would be necessary to make it fulfilling for you.

Another important factor about what we do to fulfill our purpose is that we can, in fact, practice our way to greatness and develop strengths where talents don't naturally emerge. It may not look like what you expected, though. Our little ten-year-old figure skater may not have a shot at the Olympics, but if they do enjoy the sport once the pressure of greatness is lifted, they can certainly continue skating and become a skating instructor or a performer. The artist might never make it selling their work on a large scale, but they can run a gallery or teach painting classes.

The point here is that a leisure activity *can* be polished up and fine-tuned into a life purpose activity. The key is to understand our talents and strengths and to be realistic about them.

Hard vs. Soft Skills

I'm sure you have heard the terms "hard skills" and "soft skills" before. It's important to separate your skills into these two buckets in order to understand how to connect your strengths to your passions, which we'll cover in the next chapter.

Hard skills are technical, usually job-specific abilities that are learned. These skills are measurable and teachable. Many people spend a lot of time and money acquiring these skills to excel in their work. If I gave you a test right now to measure a hard skill, I can accurately assess your proficiency and predict how well you can carry out that skill in a job setting. Some examples of hard skills are programming languages, surgical practice, graphic design, and financial analysis, among many, many others.

You might have a natural affinity for certain hard skills. If you're innately good at math, for example, you might be great at financial analysis. If it's art you're good at, you may be able to learn graphic design easily. A natural talent for a hard skill can definitely set you in the right direction, but education and instruction are still required to make it an income-producing skill. Natural inclination toward math doesn't make you a financial planner or an accountant. You need to learn the trade. Precision, patience, and a steady hand don't make you a surgeon. It's the education and supervised practice that make a great doctor, in addition to the built-in ability. You need to have some level of proficiency in hard skills to enter certain fields that is further developed through education, hands-on experience, and training.

Soft skills are less obvious. They are interpersonal or behavioral skills that are more about how you interact with others and approach tasks. While soft skills are teachable to an extent, they are harder to measure and are usually developed through experience. I would not be able to determine accurately if you would make a great psychotherapist by giving you an exam, for example. I can test your knowledge of concrete information like theories and concepts, and I may be able to tease out some soft skills by asking opinion-based, situational questions, but I would not get an accurate representation of your people skills or your openness to others in this way. Some examples of soft skills include communication and active listening, problem-solving, leadership, and time management.

Soft skills are harder to teach because, while hard skills are easier to learn if you have a natural inclination toward them, soft skills *depend* on a person's natural abilities. For example, can you imagine teaching time management to a person who has no natural sense of time and is always late? We can show this person some tips and tricks for tracking time, but it will always require effort for them to be timely and efficient.

Soft skills are way more dependent on natural ability than hard skills, and they are more transferable across industries. Most jobs require some level of communication and time management, so those who are better at certain soft skills tend to be more successful, even if their hard skills are limited. The good news, though, is that soft skills can be improved upon with reflection, feedback, and self-awareness. Although I can't teach all of the technicalities of developing soft skills in this format, I can give you some pointers.

Developing Soft Skills

Soft skills are a great way to make yourself marketable across many different fields. They help not only in the actual job but also in the interview process and in the transition to a new field. If you're a great communicator, you tend to come off as likeable. If you're receptive to feedback, you come off as teachable. If you're a great listener, you are probably a great problem-solver, too. As you can imagine, these traits are valuable in almost every field.

A great starting point for developing soft skills is learning to be curious and asking questions. If you're not used to doing this in your everyday life, that's okay. You can foster curiosity. It all starts with opening up your mind. Very often, people have their own way of doing things and live by the motto, "If it ain't broke, don't fix it."

My husband is very much like this. John could eat the same meal for dinner for the rest of his life and not complain. He likes his routines, and up until a few years ago, he preferred direct instruction over figuring things out on his own. He was very much a "just tell me what to do and I'll do it" type of guy. He loved to read and was always open to learning, but he liked using proven systems to get things accomplished.

At one point, we had a leak in the new vanity that had just been installed in our bathroom. It was seeping behind the wall and could have caused a lot of issues. It was a small job, though, and all the plumbers we knew kept saying they'd call him back when they had a moment to get to it.

John got annoyed and looked up the problem on YouTube. He figured out the tools he needed, went to Home Depot, and, with his knee pads on and iPad in hand, he got to work.

He was able to fix the pipe and the wall behind the vanity, and more important, he felt accomplished. This was the start of John's DIY ventures. Some things went well, and others not so much, like when he thought he could paint our bathroom with vaulted ceilings a dark-blue color. That was a disaster. But each time he finished a project, he learned what he's capable of and when he needed to hire help.

Most of the time, the instructions he found were pretty direct, which suited his learning style. As he did more and more projects, however, he started to sharpen his research skills. If a video or manual he found was not exactly in line with what we were dealing with, he had to piece together information from various sources to solve the problem. He did a lot of this during our RV days, because our model was new and there weren't many tutorials specific to our motorhome.

John has become so good at doing his own research, he taught himself to be a day trader. He has learned to ask the right questions, he has developed a good relationship with AI, and he has mastered the soft skills of curiosity and critical thinking, which allowed him to develop the hard skills necessary for his new trade.

Curiosity can take you to places you never even thought of. We live in a world where knowledge is free and it's possible to piece together your own career training. It all starts with asking questions. If you don't know what to ask, start with brainstorming how to improve the worst thing in your life. Whether it's a bad relationship with a co-parent or a stubborn stain on your glass cooktop, there is information out there that can help you resolve the problem. All it takes is some research.

The more research you do, the better questions you ask, and the more you sharpen your critical thinking skills. For every bit of good information out there, there is also bad information. Critical thinking means you're able to sort through the noise and pick out the meaningful information that pertains to your question.

Another good soft skill to develop is communication, both oral and written. Most careers require some form of communication, because there are either customers or coworkers or subcontractors whom you need to communicate with. If you're not a great communicator, it can be difficult to attract new business, even if you're great at what you do. People prefer to pay more for a desirable experience where they feel heard and understood than to pay less and feel like they weren't treated right, despite the end result being the same.

You can build your communication skills by becoming more self-aware. It helps to analyze a conversation after it happens to see where you feel like you communicated your thoughts, feelings, and needs effectively, and where you held back. If you do this enough, you'll probably uncover patterns of what you tend to avoid saying and the situations that cause you to overexplain or under-explain yourself. Awareness is eighty percent of the work, and once you know your patterns, it's easier to consciously adjust in the moment.

Another great tip for improving communication skills is to slow down and simplify. Don't feel the need to respond immediately. Sometimes, a well-placed "let me get back to you on that" is more effective than trying to figure out your response on the fly.

Taking a pause before responding also helps you to sort your emotions. If you're passionate and excited about something, you might overzealously promise something you can't deliver. Or if you're being asked to do something you're not looking forward to, you might be unrealistic in how you will handle it. Taking some time to think through your response to a question or a request can really help to simmer down the emotions, so you can respond with confidence and grace.

Another bit of advice I have for developing communication skills is to get feedback. You can ask a friend or coworker how you come off in certain situations or you can even record yourself on a phone call. It's a little awkward, listening to yourself ramble on, but it's insanely helpful in understanding and improving your communication style.

I used to record myself teaching my college classes. I got a ton of feedback and learned where I need to adjust. I was surprised to discover that my active listening was lacking. When a student would ask me a question, I tended to formulate the answer in my head before they were done asking, and so I would either not answer the question fully or my response would be only loosely related to what they were asking. As an introvert, I take time to sort through the information in my brain before I speak. I guess, over time, I learned to stop listening when I felt like I had enough information to get a head start on formulating my response.

Until I watched myself in action, I didn't realize I was doing this.

It was cringey for me to watch, but in my recordings, I could see the moment when I stopped paying attention to what the student was saying. After my response, I would ask, "Did that answer your question?" and they would say yes with a look on their face indicating otherwise.

I learned that, in communication, listening is just as important as talking, and my class discussions improved immensely after I made the shift to paying full attention to the full question. As a result, it took me a bit longer to come up with my answer sometimes, but I learned to communicate this with my class by saying something like, "Oh, good question! Let me think about that for a moment." Then, I would make them sit through a few seconds of awkward silence before I gave my response. My students felt heard, my responses were more complete, and I felt good because I was able to effectively communicate my needs for an extended processing time, which was received fairly well.

This leads me to the last soft skill I'd like you to learn: interpersonal and teamwork skills. Most of us have to work with other people, so we might as well make it as effective and efficient as possible. Understanding your own limitations and asking for accommodations can go a long way in improving teamwork and results.

In my example, I spent most of my life trying to hide my slow processing speed. Although most people probably didn't even realize I was doing this, it was hindering my effectiveness, because my students were not getting my full attention when they needed it. When I gave a half-formed response, they probably thought I was responding from a place of superiority, was bored of their questions, or was just brushing them off. This was not true at all!

When I realized this, I communicated my needs to my students, who were my team in the classroom. I asked for their patience as I processed the questions and gave better responses. We ended up having a much better system for discussion where I could work at my speed and they knew what I needed.

Interpersonal skills can be developed through self-awareness, knowing how you are perceived in group settings. Next time you're in a group setting where you think you can improve your interpersonal skills, pay some extra attention to how the person who you think has the best skills shows up in the group. Watch how they listen to others, how they respond, and even how they use their body to communicate.

Do they maintain eye contact with and position their body toward the person speaking? Do they appear to be engrossed in the conversation? Do they provide well-thought-out responses and contribute effectively to the discussion? These are all traits of someone who is excellent at interpersonal communication.

If you feel like you lack in any of these areas, I suggest you start by doing some journaling around how you'd like to present yourself confidently. Here is a trajectory of how you might handle implementing your new skills without feeling overwhelmed:

- Journal about the person you'd like to be, and pinpoint the areas where you need to improve. Make a list of soft skills you'd like to develop, and attach a *why* to each one. For example, if you feel like you need to maintain better eye contact during conversations, ask yourself why. What would improve about the conversation if you were better at eye contact?

- Visualize yourself as the person with excellent interpersonal skills in a group setting. See yourself doing the things you feel like you're lacking, and then journal about how you feel after your simulation. Did you end up feeling confident? Like you were able to get your point across? Like you spoke up more than you normally would? What would improve about your life, if you carried these new skills to other settings like friend groups or romantic partnerships?

- When you're in an actual group setting, start with active listening. Pay attention to what each person says, and try not to form an opinion or a response until after they're done talking. Also, don't interrupt people. Let them finish their thought and then respond from a place of understanding, rather than judgment. Many people listen just to respond. It's much better to listen to understand.

Mastering listening is the foundation for improving communication, because you begin to understand the group dynamics that you may have ignored before. Every group has its own systems and norms, and if you don't like the way your group operates, you're probably in the wrong group.

Groups function best if everyone involved is contributing effectively, listening to one another, and adhering to the norms rather than resisting them. If there is a group member who only responds from their own point of view and fails to consider the opinions of the other members, it becomes sorely obvious, and they tend to stand out as the odd man out. Checking your ego at the door and entering a group setting with a collaborative mindset goes a long way in efficiency and effectiveness.

Chapter 4 Exploration Exercises

The following exercises are intended not only to help you recognize your strengths, talents, and skills, but also to analyze how the application of them makes you feel. This sets up the groundwork for identifying passions and what naturally brings you joy. As always, please take your time with this. You may find you need more than a week to effectively reflect on your strengths. This is because we're often very critical of ourselves and it's not easy to give ourselves credit for what we're good at. The more time you spend reflecting, the more strengths you will identify.

1. Strength Journaling

Identify patterns in your everyday activities that highlight your strengths. Focus on the types of tasks that come naturally and make you feel capable.

For one week, spend ten to fifteen minutes at the end of each day reflecting on moments when you felt confident, energized, or accomplished. Write down the activities or tasks that led to those feelings.

2. Skills and Strengths Inventory

Differentiate between what you're capable of doing and what you naturally excel at and enjoy.

- Create two columns: one labeled "Hard Skills" and the other "Soft Skills." List your hard skills (e.g., software proficiency, writing) and your soft skills (e.g., empathy, leadership, problem-solving).

- Identify which skills on either side of the list you naturally excel at and how the application of these skills makes you feel.

3. **Flow State Reflection**

Flow states often occur when we are using our natural talents and working with passion. Reflecting on these moments helps pinpoint activities that align with your strengths.

Think about times when you were so absorbed in an activity, you lost track of time. Write down what you were doing, how you felt, and why you were so engaged. Try to identify the skills or talents you were using.

CHAPTER 5

Passion as a Compass

HAVE YOU EVER WORKED on something that gave you an immense sense of fulfillment and drive? You look forward to working on this thing, and even if it's part of your job, it doesn't actually feel like work. The pride you feel when you see results is intensely satisfying, and you get lost in your activity, often losing track of time.

If you've ever felt like this about a job, project, or activity, you may have experienced passion.

Defining Passion

Passion is a strong feeling of enthusiasm or excitement for something, and it's often front and center when shaping life choices, making career moves, and working on personal development.

Think about your passion as the principle underlying what you enjoy doing. It can look different based on the type of work you're doing, but the underlying principle is the same.

For example, when I was doing this deep introspective work that I'm guiding you through now, I learned that my passion is teaching. I outlined all the roles and responsibilities I've had at all the jobs I've worked, and I thought about which ones made me the happiest or most fulfilled. I realized it was when I was training others or teaching that I felt the most driven and happy.

The first job where I had the chance to assume the role of trainer was when I worked at an ice cream shop as a teenager. I loved that job in general, but I especially enjoyed it when new hires came around and I got to show them the ropes.

Fast forward a few years. After college, I worked for a Fortune 500 insurance company. It was dreadful (corporate does *not* suit me well), and out of all my jobs, I disliked this one the most. But I happened to be good at it, and as a result, I was selected to train cohorts of new hires. I enjoyed this part of the job so much, I considered branching out to the training department. At this point, however, I was already knee-deep in grad school applications, and when I was told they weren't hiring for that department, I stopped trying and made my exit.

After grad school, I became an actual teacher. I hadn't identified my passion pattern yet, but the idea of teaching psychology at the college level excited me. I did love it for a while, but eventually, things shifted within me and within the higher education system itself, which ultimately turned me off. I made my exit from that career, as well.

Concurrent with all of the above, I was pursuing entrepreneurial ventures. I tried network marketing, I excelled in real estate investing, and then, I started a successful bookkeeping company. I eventually left the teaching behind to go all in on real estate and bookkeeping.

I was happy, but something was missing. When I did my introspective work, I realized I was happiest when I was teaching others *and* successful in entrepreneurship. That's when The Mindful Waypoint—my brand, my movement—was born. The name came to me before the rest of the concept. I had heard the word *waypoint* once or twice before, and when I looked up the meaning, it really stuck with me. It means "a stop on a journey," and that's exactly how I envisioned my presence and guidance would feel to the people who would work with me.

I wanted my work to be a waypoint for those who are on their journey to self-discovery. It started as a very rough concept, of course, but the spark of genius was ignited in a singular moment one night, while I was journaling.

Once I had this idea of combining the teaching of others with entrepreneurship, an absolute flood of ideas came flowing in. My flagship method, Mindful Manifest Flow, came to me immediately, and I had the whole program mapped out in a matter of minutes. In a nutshell, it's a ten-week meditation series that teaches mindfulness and helps you surrender and align with your desires to manifest the life you desire with ease. It has taken me a while to put the course together, and as of the release of this book, it's still in the works, but I have no doubt it will be life-changing for many people.

The premise for this very book you're holding came flowing in soon after. I wasn't even finished with my own introspective work when I started outlining this book, because I knew I had stumbled upon something truly powerful. The changes I was seeing in myself and my life were amazing, and I was just bursting at the seams to share it with you, so you can experience your own transformation!

My purpose was unlocked at this point, and after completing the activities in this chapter, yours might be, too. Identifying and naming your passion is powerful work.

Flow State

I introduced the idea of a *flow state* in your reflection prompt in the previous chapter on strengths and talents. A flow state occurs when we are working on something we find immensely enjoyable. We tend to lose track of time, and we look forward to entering that state again. It happens when a passion is combined with a talent.

My first distinct memory of a flow state was when I was training new hires at the insurance company. It happened on the second or third day of training, and I got so lost in the process that I skipped right over their lunchtime. It was only when a trainee casually asked, "When's lunch today?" that I realized I was probably breaking some labor laws by having them work continuously for so many hours.

This flow state hit me so hard because there was such a contrast between my regular role with the company, which I very much disliked, and this new role. It was such a breath of fresh air, emotionally relocating me from dread and despair to hope and enjoyment, I got lost in the feeling.

I continued to enter flow states when I was teaching at the university, often holding my students past the class's end time. Yes, I was *that* professor, but it was because I got lost in the conversations while teaching a subject that I absolutely loved: psychology.

A flow state can be achieved through activities other than work, too. Some people experience flow through artistic expression, participation in sports, and even through learning new things. In order to extract the passion from the experience of the flow state, it's important to consider all aspects of the state. I will prompt you to examine the right things in your exercises at the end of this chapter.

Intrinsic vs. Extrinsic Motivation

Passion is found when your actions align with your values, skills, and intrinsic motivation. We've gone over all of these terms in detail already, except one, so let's explore it.

Intrinsic motivation is the desire to do something because it feels fulfilling, rather than doing something for external rewards (which would be *extrinsic motivation*). When we are intrinsically motivated, the motivation comes from within, and the activity itself becomes rewarding.

We're not talking about the mechanics of the activity, but rather the *reason* we are engaging in that activity. For example, the decision to exercise could be extrinsically motivated if you're doing it to lose weight or tone up, or it could be intrinsically motivated if you do it because exercise makes you feel good physically and emotionally. The extrinsic motivation comes from the tangible results you can see (changes in your appearance), and intrinsic motivation comes from things you cannot see as a result of your activity (less stress, less anxiety, etc.)

When you're living your purpose, there will be natural extrinsic motivators. There will be money if you turn your purpose into a career, there might be praise and/or fame, and there might even be competition. When there are extrinsic motivators involved, they can begin to outshine the intrinsic ones.

I worked with a coaching student named Anna, who was a psychologist. I met her through my network of colleagues at the university, where I worked in the psychology department. Anna and I met casually, but when she learned about the work I was doing, she immediately unloaded all of her feelings of burnout and stress in her career. We agreed to discuss her issues formally, so she could get the full benefit of exploring her purpose.

I often have friends and acquaintances come to me with complex problems, and I lovingly refuse to give them my unhindered full scope of advice. Of course, I try to help them through any stuck-thought processes and offer words of motivation and encouragement, but I do not attempt to do purpose work in an informal setting. It's too powerful and requires too much focus and intimacy of the sort that friends typically don't share. I also won't take them on as clients for formal work, because a coaching relationship should be set up, first and foremost, on the foundation of expertise on the coach's part, and friends will have a million different descriptors of me before they reach the word "expert."

I digress; back to Anna. Anna had been working as a psychologist for over twenty years, and she had gotten into the field for the right reasons. Helping people through mental and emotional challenges is definitely Anna's purpose-aligned work. It fits her values, her strengths, and her passion, and it is a service to others.

She started her career working with homeless youth at a non-profit. She scaled her skills and earned her doctorate in clinical psychology, and then she went into private practice. She worked for a counseling practice where she was responsible for her own list of clients. The practice took care of billing and overhead and offered some referrals.

Anna excelled in her work. She was booked to the brim with clients, and she felt extremely fulfilled by her work. She got to a point where she'd developed a preference for a certain type of client and transitioned to working exclusively with that population; she even started her own practice. She became so successful, in fact, she was often invited to speak at events that catered to professionals in her niche, and she wrote several books. It seemed as though she was stepping more and more into her purpose. On the outside, she looked like she had it all figured out, like she was meant to make strides in the world of mental health around her expertise, but internally, she was feeling burnt out and unfulfilled.

She was struggling to keep up with her clients at her practice because she was constantly pulled toward speaking at events and collaborating on projects. Her publisher was pressuring her for the next book. And her home life was suffering, as well. Did I mention she had two teenagers and a husband?

When we first met, I noticed how small her presence was. I had no idea who she was at the time, and when a colleague described her massive achievements and notoriety, I was surprised. I'd assumed someone of her stature would be a commanding presence and a big personality. She did not fit the part for me.

I became curious and started asking her questions. I was working on my professional counseling license at this point, and she offered to help me navigate the process, because she had supervised dozens of aspiring counselors over the years (the license requires 3,000 hours of supervised work).

When we started talking, she became intrigued by the work I was doing in coaching purpose-seeking women. With Anna being a top-tier psychologist, I began downplaying my own work, which I thought paled in comparison to hers. Anna kept prodding me, though, and eventually she spilled out how unsatisfied she was in her work. I was intimidated, but I did think I could help her.

You might be wondering why a psychologist with twenty years' experience would not be equipped to help herself. Well, there are two reasons in Anna's case. First, there's a difference between being able to advise others and advising yourself. You lack authority with yourself, and you're often blind to certain parts of your personality that a trained person can help bring your awareness to. That's why therapists have therapists!

The second reason Anna couldn't help herself was that her niche and her expertise revolved around survivors of domestic and sexual abuse. She was excellent at helping people with their basic needs, like safety and self-worth, but there are a few steps between that point and self-fulfillment. Her work exists toward the bottom of the hierarchy of needs, while mine exists at the very top. Humbly, I will say that her work is far more complex and intricate than mine, and I give her a lot of credit for the lives she literally saved.

It was Anna who suggested we enter into a coaching relationship, not me. I was still thrown off by the credential and experience disparity, not to mention the age gap, but I agreed to work with her.

When she described her career trajectory to me, I could pinpoint exactly where the issue was, but to be sure, I asked more questions about why she made the moves she had made. As I predicted, her motivation shifted from intrinsic to extrinsic when she began receiving new notoriety and compensation.

I asked her to recall the last time she truly felt fulfilled and at peace. At first, she said it was at her first career stop, the non-profit where she'd worked with homeless youth.

She described a simpler time, when all she had to worry about was solving one problem at a time for one person at a time. She felt good about how she was making a difference, and although she thought about her clients often, she had been able to enjoy her time off from work.

We did a comparison of her life now with the life she was living then. She was a young twenty-something with no kids, no significant other, and no responsibilities other than her work. When she went on to graduate school, the responsibilities started piling up. She got married, had kids, bought a house, etc.

I gently reminded her that she could not shed *all* of the responsibilities she'd acquired, but she certainly could shed some. She laughed and agreed she would keep her kids and her husband.

She thought harder and realized that the point in her career where she had peaked, fulfillment-wise, was when she was working for the counseling practice and became successful enough to select her client type. She liked her work, and she appreciated not having to worry about the business end of things, like bookkeeping, billing, and overhead. She decided that she hated the fame aspect of her work. She was driven purely by extrinsic motivators in the form of money and recognition during that part of her career. She found no intrinsic value to speak of.

I didn't even have to say anything more. She knew exactly which parts of her career did not suit her and went to work right away, canceling her book deal, withdrawing from several conferences, and closing up her independent practice. She joined a small counseling group, where the owner was surprised that someone with her level of success would show up on his doorstep, asking for a job, and she continued doing the work she loves.

Before setting her loose, however, I had to have the conversation about money. All those years of money flowing freely into their lives led Anna and her husband to live a lavish lifestyle. I brought Anna's attention to the fact that her income would be significantly reduced and her family would need to make adjustments. We finished our work together by coming up with a financial plan to bridge the gap between the life she had and the life she craved. Usually, this part of the process goes in the opposite direction—people tend to crave a grander life than they have—but in Anna's case, she didn't care much about the money and just wanted peace and freedom.

Anna's story is a great example of how intrinsically-motivated work can quickly become unfulfilling and cumbersome when extrinsic motivators begin to take over. When this happens, it's important to anchor into the reason we began the work in the first place, and to assess our level of fulfillment on a regular basis. (I will get into purpose maintenance in Chapter 11.)

Chapter 5 Exploration Exercises

The following activities will help you sift through what makes you feel inspired and energized to identify your true passion. This one can be a little tougher than the previous pillars we've worked on, so please take your time. Sometimes, we have to trace our patterns to identify the underlying factors.

If these activities take you more than a week, that's totally fine. In my coaching programs, we spend a disproportionate amount of time identifying passions because this is what truly sets the groundwork for living your life's purpose, so take all the time you need.

1. Journaling: The Peak Experiences

Reflect on moments in your life when you felt most fulfilled and alive. These "peak experiences" can often highlight your core passions.

- Write down as many of these moments as you can. Focus on what you were doing, who you were with, and why the experience felt so meaningful.
- Analyze these experiences for common themes (your passion pattern) that might reveal your passions linked to your purpose.

2. Childhood Reflection

Think back to when you were a child or teenager. What activities or dreams made you excited or happy at that time? Often, the things we were naturally drawn to as children can indicate deeper passions that we may have forgotten or ignored, as we grew up.

Write down these activities and explore how they align with your current interests.

3. Mood Tracking

Over the course of a week, keep a journal of your daily activities, and note your emotional responses. Pay attention to which activities make you feel energized, happy, or fulfilled, and which ones drain your energy.

By tracking your emotional responses, you can identify patterns that pinpoint what you are most passionate about.

4. Flow State Analysis

Go back to your Flow State exercise from Chapter 4. Consider the experience you wrote about and identify the following:

- If you could recreate that flow state right now, how would you do it?

- Is there anything specific about the environment that contributed to your flow state? For example: location, level of supervision, freedom for creativity, etc.

- What title would you give yourself if your job involved the work you were performing in your flow state?

- Who were you serving with the work you were doing?

Now, see if you can come up with a few more times you recall entering a flow state, and answer the questions above for each.

CHAPTER 6

The Impact of Life Experiences

LOOKING TO THE PAST for answers about ourselves can be a tough process. It often involves reopening some wounds that didn't heal properly and coming to terms with where you've been and where you are. This process can take several years or even decades, and I highly recommend you explore yourself in this manner.

I, unfortunately, am unable to bring you fully through that journey in this format. Exploration of your past and how it relates to identifying your purpose requires one-on-one interaction, something I work on with my clients in coaching.

What I can do for you now, however, is ask some guiding questions and prompt a thought process that will help you identify where you're going. I can also give you some instruction on how to recover from your past, but please do not use this as a substitute for therapy.

I do recommend being in a good headspace for this part of your reading. Ideally, you'd be in a good headspace for all of your introspective work, but reflecting on the past and attempting to reverse the consequences of it requires some extra level-headedness.

Subconscious Reprogramming

Who you are is a reflection of where you've been. And if you haven't healed the old you, there are probably some remnants of that identity left in your personality. Healing requires some rough, invasive reflection on our past, and oftentimes a new person emerges. This new person might be unrecognizable to people from the past, and a lot of relationship loss will occur. I daresay, losing relationships is inevitable if the work is done right.

This happens because the old relationships supported and encouraged the old person. When we actually heal our old wounds, we shed old habits and viewpoints that we do not want to take with us to our future. This happens frequently to recovering addicts. A lot of relationships are formed around addiction, and most of them dissolve when the addiction is no longer the focus of the person's life.

The major barrier to proper healing is that our subconscious becomes very comfortable, living in the habits of the version of ourselves we're trying to evolve from. I'd like to take some time now to explain some metaphysical stuff that will hopefully help you fit some pieces together in the "why am I like this" puzzle.

There are two influences on your thinking and behaviors: the conscious mind and the subconscious mind. The conscious mind is the one you control, but it is greatly influenced by the subconscious, which is your invisible passenger in life. It lives in your brain and holds deeply rooted beliefs about who you are and what you deserve. It's that nasty little voice that tells you you're not good enough or that things are going too well, and the other shoe will be dropping soon.

Your subconscious determines what your external reality will look like, because it provides the foundation to all of your thoughts and motivations. It takes in its information from your experiences and creates its own self-concept. This information comes from your parents' behaviors and words you witnessed as a child, your own experiences, your perception of what others think of you, and where you come from in life.

When you blend all that data together, the subconscious knows exactly what you deserve and what to expect. The problem is that the subconscious is like a very basic computer and only knows how to take an average of all this data, rather than analyzing it thoroughly.

For example, if you witnessed your parents constantly worrying about money, like I did, you grew up thinking money was scarce and you would never have enough of it. When you became an adult, maybe you got a good job and began bringing in decent money, but it seemed like there was still never enough. You continued to strive for more, and then, when more would come, the lack cycle would continue, where you spent the money just as quickly as it came in.

The subconscious convinces you to spend the money on things you "need" like a nice house and nice cars because that's what the money's for, after all. Then, when you're still living paycheck to paycheck despite the consistent increases in income, barely able to afford your bills, your subconscious is, like, "See? I told you there's never enough money!"

The money goes out as fast as it comes in because your subconscious convinces you to increase your spending. It needs to keep you in a place of lack and scarcity in order to maintain its belief. And the subconscious *loves* to maintain its belief system. It needs to prove to you that there's never enough money because that's how it was programmed.

There's only one way to reprogram the subconscious. You have to feed it contradicting data until the average of everything it knows is tipped in a favorable direction. If you do this passively, it takes a very long time. Passive reprogramming requires experiences in the direction we want the scales tipped. In our money-lack example, your salary would need to outpace your subconscious's spending advice in order to convince the subconscious that there is, in fact, enough money for you to feel secure. But by the time this happens, you're probably living in a giant mansion and have a million dollars' worth of cars. Most people never get to this point.

The other option is active reprogramming. Once you understand how the subconscious operates, you can feed it new information through your thoughts and actions via your conscious mind. Switching your mindset from the programming of financial lack to abundance requires *conscious* application of logic. "If I don't buy this expensive car, I can put money away in an investment account and it will grow."

The subconscious is confused at this point and telling you it's a waste of time. Then, you consciously resist buying the car and invest your money, ignoring your subconscious's protest, and your money does, in fact, grow. Then, you begin to feel financially secure because your subconscious has no choice but to change its tune. The new data has trumped its old programming, and the average has shifted.

This is because your subconscious just learned a new behavior. You'll have to make the conscious decision to spend less over and over again, of course, before convincing the subconscious that saving is better than spending. Once that's done, though, the saving will become the subconscious behavior and will no longer require the mental effort of a conscious decision.

You can also actively reprogram using words. The subconscious believes what it hears, especially when the words are repeated and stated with conviction. This works even better when you bring in gratitude. Affirmations are a great way to undo unuseful programming.

Here's how affirmations can be used effectively for subconscious reprogramming:

Choosing the Right Affirmations

- Identify Limiting Beliefs: The first step is to recognize the negative or limiting beliefs you want to reprogram. These could be thoughts like "I'm not good enough," "I don't deserve success," or "I'm bad with money." It might be helpful to assess where these beliefs come from, so that you can identify where the incorrect thinking originated.

  For example, if you believe all relationships are doomed to fail because you grew up with a parent who often had relationship troubles, remind yourself that that's only one example of what love looks like. There are tons of people in the world who have successful relationships, and you are worthy of love. You have only one source of data for this belief you've hung your hat on, and you have allowed it to define you. This is bad science; you need more data.

Look at other people in your life and what their relationships look like. If those are all bad, too, maybe you're in the wrong environment. Look at the world at large and realize that it's statistically normal to have a healthy lifelong relationship with a partner and your soulmate does exist somewhere out there.

Try to go through a process like this for each limiting belief you identify.

- Create Positive Replacements: Transform these limiting beliefs into positive, present-tense affirmations that represent the belief you want to hold. For example, replace, "I'm not good enough" with "I am worthy of success and happiness" or "I am capable of achieving my goals."
- Focus on Core Desires: Make sure your affirmations align with the life you want to manifest. If your goal is to attract financial abundance, create affirmations like, "I attract wealth easily and effortlessly."

Repetition and Consistency

- Daily Practice: Repeating affirmations regularly is key to reprogramming the subconscious. Saying them once or twice isn't enough. The subconscious absorbs information through consistent repetition over time, so it's important to say your affirmations daily, and ideally multiple times a day.
- Create a Mantra: Choose an affirmation to carry with you throughout the day, and repeat it to yourself several times as you go about your usual life.

- Morning and Evening Rituals: As a routine, use affirmations first thing in the morning and right before bed, because your brain is most receptive to new information during these times. The subconscious is more easily accessed when you're in a relaxed state, like during the transition between wakefulness and sleep.

Emotion and Visualization

- Engage Emotion: The subconscious mind responds strongly to emotions. When using affirmations, it's important to really feel the positive emotions associated with the statements. For example, when saying, "I am worthy of love," try to feel the warmth and security that comes with being loved and valued.

    This takes practice. Slowing down and pausing between affirmations to allow for an emotional response is necessary. Recite the affirmation, then pause for a few breaths and invite the emotion to enter. If no emotion comes up, keep practicing that affirmation, and try to incorporate some visualization, as I describe in the next step, to see if that will elicit an emotional response.

- Combine with Visualization: Visualizing yourself living out the truth of your affirmations strengthens their effect. If your affirmation is, "I am confident and successful," visualize yourself confidently achieving your goals and thriving in your new life. Try to imagine the you who believes the affirmation. How do you look? How do you hold yourself? How do you feel? Visualize the confidence and the joy radiating from you. This should help elicit the emotion.

Writing Affirmations

- **Write Them Down:** Writing your affirmations by hand further engrains them in your subconscious. The act of writing adds another layer of reinforcement to the reprogramming process.

- **Affirmation Cards:** Create affirmation cards or sticky notes, and place them where you'll see them throughout the day—on your mirror, desk, or phone. Seeing them regularly reminds your subconscious of these new beliefs.

Present Tense and Positivity

- **Use Present Tense:** Affirmations should always be framed as if the desired outcome is happening right now, not in the future. This tells your subconscious that the belief is already your reality. For example, say, "I am abundant" instead of "I will be abundant."
- **Keep it Positive:** Avoid negative language or focusing on what you don't want. Instead of saying, "I am not afraid of failure," say, "I embrace success and growth." Do not use the word "not."

Belief and Commitment

- **Believe in the Process:** For affirmations to work, it's crucial to believe they are working even before you see external results. Initially, the affirmations might feel untrue or awkward, especially if they contradict long-standing limiting beliefs. With consistency,

however, the subconscious will begin to accept these new beliefs as truths.
- Commit to Long-Term Practice: Subconscious reprogramming takes time. It requires dedication and patience, especially if you're addressing deeply-ingrained beliefs. When you commit to daily affirmation practices, you'll start to notice gradual shifts in your thoughts, feelings, and behaviors. Acknowledging and reflecting on these shifts can help reinforce the belief that the process is working, so check in with yourself regularly, and look for proof in your mindset, your thought processes, and in your external world.

Here are some examples of affirmations to get you started. You can play with these or come up with your own. Just remember to keep them in the present-tense and positive (no "not" statements).

"I am worthy of success and happiness."

"I attract positive opportunities effortlessly."

"I am confident in my abilities and trust myself."

"Money flows to me easily and abundantly."

"I am deserving of love, respect, and kindness."

"I am aligned with my purpose and live it daily."

Turning Pain Into Purpose

Unfortunately, subconscious reprogramming isn't enough to recover from your past. It's a great way to change the narrative of where you come from and who you are, but it does not rid you of your pain or trauma.

The actual healing work is done by facing your demons. The best way to accomplish this, especially if the trauma runs deep, is by starting supportive therapy. I can't say this enough: everyone needs therapy. The issue is, though, not every therapist is the same, and people expect unrealistic outcomes from therapy. Many people enter therapy and quit soon after because they feel no benefit, but nine out of ten times, it was just not the right fit.

Of course, I cannot offer you therapy in this format. What I can do, though, is provide some general guidance for turning your trauma into something useful. Your past is your greatest teacher, and it often feels good to help those who are affected by experiences you've already been through.

One main facet of purpose is using your own experiences. When you've been through something significant and have come out on the other side, you'll often feel drawn to people who are going through something similar. It's usually a synergistic exchange, with both the person who has been through it and the person going through it benefiting from the relationship.

A great example of turning pain into purpose is recovering addicts who enter the field of addiction and recovery. They've been through the process, and they know what it feels like. They are uniquely suited to understanding the struggle the recovering person is going through. They are also much more relatable, because the patient sees them as an example of what's possible for their own future.

Turning pain into purpose takes time and requires self-healing, first and foremost. Self-reflection is necessary, and it helps to find the meaning within the experience. Viktor Frankl, a Holocaust survivor and psychiatrist, emphasized in his book *Man's Search for Meaning* that humans can endure almost any hardship as long as they find meaning in it. It's finding the meaning in a horrific experience that helps us shift from suffering to healing.

Therapy, of course, helps to process trauma and to understand the hidden messages within the experience. Trauma-focused cognitive-behavioral therapy, or TF-CBT, is a great choice of therapeutic modality for resolving trauma. TF-CBT encourages reflection by helping to identify negative, unhelpful thought patterns. With the guidance of your therapist, you can start recognizing these patterns in your thinking and replace them with healthier thoughts.

Working through trauma using reflection can be a good starting point. Reflection in the form of journaling, meditation, writing about the trauma as a third-person narrative, gratitude practice, and artistic expression are some great examples of what you can do to unravel trauma.

Let's go through each of these in some detail so you can understand the various ways in which you can help yourself. You can put your own spin on these techniques and make them resonate with you and your needs.

Journaling. Writing down your thoughts, feelings, and experiences can help you reflect on what has happened and gain insight into your emotions. By putting your thoughts on paper, you create space for deeper understanding and emotional release.

Use specific prompts to guide your journaling, such as:

- What emotions am I feeling right now, and why?
- What lesson can I learn from this experience?

- How has this situation impacted me, and how can I grow from it?

Mindfulness Meditation. Practicing mindfulness meditation allows you to observe your thoughts and feelings without judgment. This practice allows you to reflect on your emotions and experiences more clearly.

Mindfulness encourages living in the present, which can help you accept things as they are without trying to resist or change them. Observing without judgment, a key element in mindfulness meditation, allows us to accept reality and see things as they truly are. This builds the foundation for creating change and healing.

Narrating Trauma in the Third-Person. Writing helps to sort your thoughts and identify elements of yourself that might be suppressed deep down inside your consciousness. Sometimes it helps to put some emotional distance between you and the trauma, which is why third-person writing can be helpful. By stepping outside of your direct involvement in the story, you can observe your trauma more objectively.

This method also puts you in control over the narrative, making it easier to confront difficult emotions and memories. You can write this in any style, and there could be elements in the story that are not based in reality, if they empower your position and help you confront the difficult feelings associated.

Gratitude Practice. By practicing gratitude, you shift your focus from negative to positive. There is always something to be grateful for, even in the toughest of times. Gratitude journaling, for example, allows you to reflect on the good in your life, even while there is pain. This helps you realize that, while some things are difficult, there are still blessings to be acknowledged, and it feeds your subconscious new data: *I have abundance and positivity around me.*

When you consciously practice gratitude daily, you'll begin to change your entire outlook on life, and your internal dialogue will improve, too.

Artistic Expression. Using art, music, or creative writing to express and reflect on your emotions can help bring repressed feelings to the surface, allowing for deeper reflection and acceptance.

Much like writing, channeling your pain into creativity allows you to reflect on the trauma and process the emotions, because you've put them in a place external to yourself, where your logical mind can interpret the information from a new point of view.

I want you to take the healing journey seriously. Your true life's purpose will not be revealed to you and life will not be as enjoyable as it can be if you remain unhealed. Trying to live your purpose with an unhealed past is kind of like putting a cast on a broken bone that needs to be reset. Sure, it might fuse back together, but it's out of place and will likely cause pain and discomfort in the future.

Many of us (myself included) have done this at some point. It's a tactile strategy that is useful in fight-or-flight mode: we can quickly mend the issue, slap a smile on our faces, and keep going because we don't have time to stop and process. This strategy has a time and a place for its usefulness, but this is not a permanent solution. We have to return to the trauma and process it.

Those broken bones need care. You need to access the source of the pain and put things back where they should be. Trauma is healed by feeling it, reflecting on it, trying to make sense of it, and finally, leaving it alone to heal once everything is back in its place.

Many times, the healing process itself will reveal new opportunities and new motivations, pushing you toward your life's purpose. When my dad died, I started to see how I had been living my life according to others' expectations. It was through my grieving and healing process that I realized I needed to get out of the bubble I had been living in.

Without much thought, I quit my job, sold everything I owned, and moved into an RV, which has all led me to this moment as I sit here, writing the very book you're reading, in the middle of Napa Valley at 5:00 a.m. My healing process opened up opportunities and allowed me to see things more clearly. Now I get to live my purpose, which is helping you find your purpose.

Chapter 6 Exploration Exercises

The following activities are meant to help you assess your experiences and help pinpoint any unhealed areas of trauma that lie within you. Sometimes, you might not realize there is unhealed trauma, and you might be surprised by what comes up in this reflection.

The goal is to uncover anything that needs healing. If/when you do find these areas, I encourage you to use some of the strategies listed in the prior section to help analyze and heal the trauma. And, of course, please seek professional help if the emotions ever get to be too much.

1. Triggers Journal

Over the course of a week, pay attention to moments when you feel triggered or have an intense emotional reaction (anger, sadness, anxiety, etc.). Write down what triggered you, how you felt, and any immediate thoughts or memories that surfaced.

After collecting several entries, look for patterns. Ask yourself:

- What specific situations or people tend to trigger me?
- Do these triggers remind me of any past experiences, especially from childhood or previous relationships?
- Could my intense reactions be linked to unresolved trauma?

2. **Childhood Memory Exercise**

Close your eyes and take yourself back to your childhood. Reflect on moments when you felt vulnerable, hurt, or misunderstood.

Picture yourself at different ages and ask:

- When did I first feel scared, hurt, or alone?
- Are there moments where I wished someone had stepped in to help me, but no one did?
- Is there a particular memory that stands out as unresolved or still charged with emotion?

After visualizing these memories, write about any experiences that stand out, especially those that still bring up strong emotions. Think about whether any unresolved feelings from childhood are impacting you today.

3. **Revisiting Old Wounds**

Write about a difficult or painful time in your life that you rarely think about or actively avoid discussing. This could be a specific event, relationship, or period of time.

As you write, answer the following questions:

- Why don't I think about or talk about this experience?
- What emotions were tied to this event? (e.g., shame, sadness, anger, fear, etc.)
- Are there still unresolved emotions tied to this event that I haven't fully processed?
- How does this past experience affect my current relationships, beliefs, or behaviors?

After writing, reflect on whether this experience still holds emotional weight. Consider whether you have truly healed or if there are lingering feelings (anger, grief, shame) that still need attention.

CHAPTER 7

Understanding Your Needs

WHY IS IT THAT WHEN we accommodate our own needs and do things in a way that is conducive to our success, people with different needs judge us? There is a resistance to accepting a new way of doing things, even if the outcome is the same or better as doing it the traditional way.

If I had a dollar for every "must be nice" comment I got when I first started my business and worked from home, I could have closed that business and made a living off telling people I work from home.

The fact of the matter is that a quiet and comfortable workspace was a need for me at the time. It still is, actually. I don't thrive in an office setting. I don't do well when socializing is a requirement to fit in. I prefer to work alone in my own space, where I could make a sandwich whenever I please.

Your needs are immensely important when considering a career or fulfillment-inducing activity, because your nervous system is calmer when you're doing something that honors your own individual needs. When you're taking care of yourself, you are infinitely more creative, productive, and efficient.

Preferences for Productivity

We all have different needs and different ways in which we thrive. Some people prefer being out of their personal environment to get work done. I knew many people in college who could not study in their dorm rooms and would need to do their work in the library.

If they tried working in their dorm rooms, they would get distracted by people in the hallway and experience FOMO because others were socializing. Or they would turn the TV on for a five-minute break that lasted for hours. Or their bed would call to them and they would wake up the next morning not knowing what happened. The library was full of people doing the same thing they were trying to do, so they felt less distracted, and fitting into the social scene meant burying their face in a laptop.

I, on the other hand, preferred to study in my room. I was never particularly interested in participating in what other people were doing. There could be a party next door and I would be annoyed with the noise more than anything. My roommate was the type of person who would be itching to join the party. She needed to study in the library. I liked to be in my own space, where I felt comfortable and things were predictable and familiar. To me, the library was too exotic. There were always different people (I'm a people watcher, so this was *very* distracting for me), you could never find the same open spot twice, and when I saw someone with a Starbucks, I would immediately be craving one, too.

I realized that most environmental preferences are based on personality. Those who tended to be more extroverted and social liked studying in the library, and those who were more introverted liked studying in their rooms.

The same pattern probably exists in these peoples' careers. The ones who studied in the library thrive on social interaction in their work. Whether it's from customers, clients, or coworkers, they need to have human connection to feel satisfied. The ones who studied in their rooms likely prefer to work alone and dread the interactions.

This, of course, is a very simplistic conclusion to draw, and not all extroverted people studied in the library. The point I'm trying to make is that preferences for work environments and the need for certain conditions in order to be productive and satisfied are largely based on personality.

Personality as an Indicator of Needs

Much of your personality is based on genetics. Psychological studies have found that infant temperament is a precursor to personality, and we can predict what a person will be like as an adult based on how they are as a baby. This means the foundation of who we are is something we were born with. Of course, there are aspects of personality that are a result of our environment and things we've been exposed to, but broad traits like introvertedness versus extrovertedness appear to be genetic.

Regardless of where they originated, personality traits can be indicative of how you work best, what type of environment suits you, and the work conditions necessary for you to feel fulfilled and productive. Our personalities are relatively stable after we enter adulthood, so if you're not familiar with your own needs and preferences yet, it's not too late to get to know yourself! It will probably bring you a lot of clarity as to why you are the way you are.

There are tons of personality assessments out there, and many of them are backed by scientific theories. Some well-known and well-researched ones include the Myers-Briggs Type Indicator (MBTI), Big Five Personality Test, and the Enneagram of Personality. There are others like the Minnesota Multiphasic Personality Inventory (MMPI), which is primarily used in clinical diagnosis, and the Rorschach Inkblot Test, which has lost some credibility over the years due to the subjective nature of the test.

The study of personality dates back to ancient times, where Hippocrates attempted to classify personality types based on the Four Humors theory in 400 BC, and personality assessment can be traced back to the early 1900s, when psychological testing was born. Since then, it has been widely studied and is considered scientific.

My favorite personality test is the MBTI. I was first introduced to it when I was in college during training for a leadership group I participated in. I remember being blown away by how accurate my description was and how much better I understood myself after taking that test. I used to introduce myself as "Izabela, INTJ," which is my personality type.

The MBTI consists of multiple-choice questions where you are asked to select your preference in specific situations. The test measures your decision-making preferences based on personality across four dichotomies: introversion (I) vs. extroversion (E), sensing (S) vs. intuition (N), thinking (T) vs. feeling (F), and judging (J) vs. perceiving (P). Each dichotomy is a range, so, based on your answers, you will fall somewhere between the two poles, indicating an affinity for one end of the spectrum and the associated trait, represented by a letter.

This results in sixteen different personality types, and the various combinations of letters indicate different traits. Some people find themselves at the center of a dichotomy, meaning they are a relatively even balance between the two poles. Usually, this person should look into both personality descriptions they could fall under. One tends to resonate more than the other.

For example, I am an INTJ through and through, but my J is not super strong, while my I is. I've taken the assessment before where I've gotten a P instead of a J, but when I read the description for INTP, I was like, "Nope, not me."

A few other examples of personality assessments: The Big Five considers personality across five different spectrums: Openness, Conscientiousness, Extraversion, Agreeableness, and Neuroticism (the letters spell OCEAN); you fall somewhere on the spectrum for each trait. The Enneagram Test focuses on motivations and fears based on personality. There are nine personality types, and each one has a core motivation and a fear associated.

These are just a few of the assessments available; several other options exist in many different forms. Some are geared specifically toward career development, while others are more general, and some are strictly used for clinical evaluation through a psychologist. It's quite an interesting branch of psychology.

Recently, I've been really interested in Human Design, which is a bit more abstract than the research-based assessments I just mentioned. Human Design is based on your birth chart rather than responses to questions. It combines astrology, chakra systems, and quantum physics to describe an individual's energetic tendencies. It's a bit more woo-woo than what I'm used to in my study of psychology, but I've been exploring this self-knowledge system, and this stuff fascinates me! I've been coming around to the more spiritual and metaphysical sides of things lately, and I kind of love it here.

I highly recommend playing with a few of these personality assessments. I believe there is value in each of them and getting results from several sources can help stitch together a dynamic view of who you are and what drives you.

Needs and Purpose

So, what do you do with all this information about yourself? Well, like any good scientist, you will take the information you've gathered and apply it to something useful. Once you understand your personality, you have a much better grasp of what you will need to feel fulfilled, how you best operate, and what you're here to do.

The most important thing to note is that your core needs will not change, no matter how much you try to push yourself. As an adult, your personality is relatively stable, and it's encoded in your emotional wiring. Pushing yourself to behave in a way that does not suit your personality is unsustainable long term, and it comes with resistance.

It's easy to get caught up in comparing yourself to others and assuming, if you just did what they do, you would be successful, too. This could not be further from the truth, though. We are all equipped with our own unique gifts and talents that suit our individual needs.

I fell into this trap, myself, recently. I am on social media daily, promoting my business and connecting with people, so I see a ton of different personalities in people who run businesses similar to mine. I caught myself spiraling one day, watching one woman's content. She's so confident and just so brilliantly herself. She doesn't care what others think. She dresses in unique outfits, says exactly what's on her mind, and just generally has a wonderful, loud confidence about her.

She's very successful. And I don't mean just flashy-on-Instagram successful. I've met this woman in real life, and she's the real deal. I found myself thinking, *I could never be that loud and audacious, so I guess that level of success is not for me.*

Another woman I follow has managed to build her business purely on social media in a matter of a few months. She shows up regularly, talking to the camera on Instagram Lives for thirty-plus minutes, just spewing great advice on how to build a social media presence. She has such great charisma, which she can deliver on the fly. Again, *I would be so much more successful if I could just turn on my camera and talk so well.*

I caught myself, though. And I journaled heavily on this topic. It's easy to get swept up by the comparisons and disregard your own strengths because someone else has shiny new features that you are lacking. But you know what's also true? The two women I just described—they don't have each other's strengths. The unique one doesn't jump on Lives and talk endlessly in a captivating and valuable way. And the charismatic one doesn't show up, dancing around in a hot-pink fluffy jacket and thigh-high boots.

They each have tapped into their own personalities and shown up authentically. They don't try to imitate someone else. It wouldn't work if they did. When I came to this realization in my journaling, just for good measure, I imagined myself dancing on camera in a hot-pink jacket and thigh-high boots, and I almost spit out my tea. It's not me.

I started to understand that I have my own unique strengths and style that others cannot imitate. I'm still working to pinpoint exactly who I am in the social media space, but since I started being more authentic and stopped watching others, I feel a lot more at ease. Staying consistent is easier *and* it's more fun. I used to dread posting on social media, but now I love it. I love the people I'm attracting, and I love expressing myself in a way that feels true to myself.

I now understand that success doesn't come to the loudest person in the room. It comes to the most authentic person. We are magnetic to people who resonate with our style and our message, and this can only happen when we are being ourselves.

Your purpose *must* be in alignment with who you are. Pushing yourself to be more like someone else when it does not feel authentic will actually repel people from you. Inauthenticity can be sensed. And it is a turnoff.

Now, there is a nuanced difference between pushing yourself out of your comfort zone and pushing yourself to be something you're not. It can be confusing to determine if something is in alignment with your purpose but just unfamiliar, versus something that's out of alignment and inauthentic. The best way to tell the difference is to explore how it makes you feel. And if it's still not clear, try it and see how it goes. If it's a no, you will feel it right away.

I like to use a point of reference to see how a new idea feels to me. My newest reference point is the hot-pink jacket and thigh-high boots. I start by visualizing that image, which is a hard no in my body. I then visualize the thing I am considering expanding into.

For example, I recently started thinking about starting a coaching community. At first, I thought, *That's not me,* but when I put some more thought into it and how I could do it in an authentic way, I realized maybe it does feel aligned. When compared to the pink jacket, it actually felt good. This idea definitely feels out of my comfort zone but in an exciting and expansive way.

I also explored recently the idea of coming out with a YouTube series sharing lessons in Mindful Manifestation. It felt okay to me, so I tried it. I recorded a couple of episodes, posted them, and realized it's not right at this point in my journey. So, I deleted them quietly and moved on. No harm, no foul. Sometimes it's worth a shot to see if something is aligned. If it's not, just adjust and keep going.

The more you explore your needs and try out new ideas, the better you will understand what truly suits you. The only way to get better acquainted with your needs and how you operate is to try things out. I'm sorry, there's no easier way. A personality assessment can point you in the right direction, but it can't tell you whether or not you will flop on YouTube. You have to try it. But it doesn't even stop there.

When you push yourself to try something new and it fails, you can't just sweep it under the rug and pretend it never happened. To truly know yourself and to make these decisions more easily in the future, you also have to assess what went wrong. It could have been misalignment or it could have been misexecution. It can be challenging to be honest with yourself following a failure.

Here are some prompts to get you started:

- Did this decision reflect my true values and personality, or was I trying to be someone I'm not?
- Did I feel off when I made this decision? Was there resistance in my mind or in my environment?
- If I did this again with more support, a different strategy, or at a different time, would it feel different?
- Did I fear being seen, failing, or succeeding? If so, how did fear influence my actions or the way I approached it, both mentally and logistically?
- Was this a "no" from my soul or a "not yet" from the Universe? Am I being redirected or did I try to control the timeline of my journey?

Exploring the Needs of Your Past Self

Sometimes, purpose can be found in serving a past version of yourself. We talked about this in the last chapter about experiences, but it's also true about needs. If you think back to times when your needs were unmet, could you be the person who meets those needs for someone who is similar to the person you once were?

Our past, whether good or bad, can be a gift to the well-being of someone else. Using our own pain to heal the pain in another person is life-changing.

The pain you once felt and the needs that went unmet may have faded away for you, but the trauma still exists in the world. And you have the unique power to help heal it. If your need to be seen and heard was ever unmet, you may be invaluable to people who are silenced or forced to shrink themselves. Maybe your purpose lies in helping others find their voice.

If you've ever felt unsafe in your circumstances due to lack of resources, maybe you're best suited to work in urban planning or social services, to help others who are in a situation like the one from your past.

Or maybe you are meant to serve those who feel like the outsider or black sheep because their need to belong is not being met. Building community for people who feel like they don't fit in could be the purpose-driven work you're looking for.

As I write this, I'm becoming more and more convinced that I need to create a community. I've often felt like I don't belong, even before my friends turned their backs on me, and now I feel like I'm being called to gather the out-of-the-box thinkers and create a space for sharing creativity, business, and general support. Stay tuned for the development of this, because I feel a strong calling toward it.

I believe that nothing is random. The experiences we have are necessary to prime us for the work we're meant to do and the difference we're meant to make. Unfortunately, most people close off the piece of themselves that was once in pain and never revisit it. They think, *I was able to get myself out of that situation, so the people who are there now can, too.* While this may be true, wouldn't it have been helpful to find someone to lend you a helping hand in your time of need? Wouldn't it have been a relief to land in a safety net?

Be that safety net for someone else. Trust me, it will heal parts of you that you didn't even know were still unhealed.

Chapter 7: Exploration Exercises

These reflection exercises are meant to help you tap into your needs and use them as a foundation for a better understanding of your life's purpose. You can't create from a place of force or inauthenticity. My goal here is to help you align with ease and truth, so your impact on the world feels like a natural flow of ideas and implementation. As always, take your time, and return to these as often as you need to.

1. **Need Mapping Visualization**

    Close your eyes. Imagine you're walking through your ideal day. This should not be a fantasy, but rather a deeply fulfilling, ideal life. Pay attention to the details: How do you start your day? What kind of environment are you in? Who's with you? How do you feel in your body? Tune into the *energy* of the day, not the tasks.

    Afterward, reflect on:

    - What emotional needs were being met in that vision? (e.g., freedom, peace, connection, excitement, clarity)
    - What physical or relational needs stood out?
    - What part of your current life is *meeting those needs*? What part isn't?

2. **Needs-to-Purpose Bridge Exercise**

List three to five core needs you've historically felt were unmet (e.g., to feel safe, seen, creative, useful, connected, in control, autonomous, understood). Now ask yourself for each one:

- What did I do to try to meet this need, growing up?
- When did I start realizing this need mattered to me?
- How does this need show up in what I care about now?
- Could this need be a clue to who I'm meant to help, create for, or advocate for?

Then, finish with this prompt:
"If I built something that honored this need, for me and for others, it might look like..."

3. Personality Alignment Inventory

Draw a simple two-column chart labeled: "My Personality Trait" on one side and "My Life/Work Honors This By..." on the other. Then fill it in with traits like:

- I'm introverted—I build in solo creative time
- I'm detail-oriented—I take on in project-based work
- I'm empathic—I've created a space that is nurturing and is not emotionally toxic
- I love learning—I structure in time for personal growth

Once complete, reflect on where your personality and your needs are honored and where they are suppressed in your life. If you're having trouble filling in the second column, that's a major signal that you're forcing and not aligning.

In order to show up as the authentic version of yourself, you must create a life that's suited to your needs. Where can you make changes?

CHAPTER 8

The Intersection of Purpose and Service

I HOPE THE INTROSPECTIVE work we've done so far has been helpful. Now, it's time to look beyond yourself and explore the last component of the Purpose Activation Blueprint: service to others. Although finding purpose is a deeply intimate and personal journey, it requires some level of giving back. You've been blessed with a gift that will bring you immense joy and happiness, but the deal is that you need to share that gift with the world.

Service to Others

I'm sure you've experienced the good feelings associated with helping someone in need. As a result of millions of years of evolution, we're quite literally programmed genetically to help our neighbors. Our prehistoric ancestors could only survive if they lived in groups and worked together to help one another get by.

To feel immense satisfaction and joy from living your purpose, you need to figure out a way to share yourself and be of service to others. This looks different for everyone. Extroverted people flourish by being the center of attention and feed off the energy of being social. Others (like me) prefer some time in isolation, and although being social and projecting ourselves out into the world can be fun and rewarding from time to time, we need to rest and recharge.

The extroverted person and I could have a similar life purpose, though. Let's consider how an event I organized would look, compared to one by the woman in the pink jacket from Chapter 7.

My day would start with a warm welcome from me and some inspiring words about overcoming doubts. We would dive into deep introspection, maybe do some energy work and meditation, followed by an enlightening and moving keynote on the topic of fear of being seen. We'd end with a nice, quiet dinner while soft music played. Then, we'd all be in bed by 9:00 p.m.

The woman in the pink jacket would probably start her event off by arriving in a show-stopping outfit. She would hype up her audience, she would inspire, she would awe, and she would do it all loudly. Her keynote would be about embracing who you are and unapologetically showing up in a true and authentic way. No one would have time to eat dinner, because all of her attendees would be chit-chatting and hyping one another up. And her night would end with a dance party that goes into the wee hours.

Our purpose is similar—to inspire women to lead with authenticity—but our delivery is very, very different, and the people we attract will benefit from our individual style of teaching and coaching. Neither of us is wrong or ineffective; we just use different talents and strengths to get across the same message.

Service to others looks very different from one person to another. For example, an accountant's or a graphic designer's service to others is obvious: they provide a direct service to the customer. An artist (painter, dancer, etc.)

shares their passion and purpose with the world by putting their art on display or sharing it with others in some way.

Despite the means and methods of sharing, allowing your purposeful work to benefit others is what drives fulfillment. There's a deep sense of satisfaction when your direct work betters the lives of others.

Purpose Beyond the Self

A major block in manifesting the life of your dreams is self-centeredness. People who cannot see beyond their own desires energetically block the flow of abundance and so cannot align with their true purpose. Finding purpose works most effectively when your intentions align with the greater good and are not focused solely on self-interest. Don't get me wrong. It is okay to (and you should) consider the benefits you get from living for your purpose, like money, notoriety, or recognition, but there must also be a desire to include others somewhere in there, too.

When you're overly focused on personal gain, you're operating from a place of scarcity and fear, because you're acting as if there is not enough to go around and you want all of it for yourself. This blocks the flow of abundance, and opportunities will be repelled from you. Instead, it is much better to think about how you can share your abundance with the world. When you're open to sharing, you are creating space for more abundance because you're showing that you are capable of receiving, holding, and distributing prosperity.

Let me give you an example. When my dad was sick, I learned mindfulness meditation as a way to relieve stress. I started practicing every day, and slowly, mindfulness crept into my daily awareness. When I paired this practice with journaling (from which this book was born!), I started to have the ability to process each situation in the present and put out of my mind everything that has happened in the past and everything I feared in the future. This helped me get through the long nights at hospitals and deal with unanswered medical questions.

When my dad passed away and I entered the grieving process, I realized just how powerful mindfulness is. I felt weirdly in control of my emotions, and I could pinpoint exactly when I needed to rest. I tried to follow the cues of my body and mind, and I allowed myself to be guided by my needs.

When I was in the thick of grieving, I received a "download" one night. This has happened to me a few times now, and it's basically a flood of ideas that comes rushing in seemingly out of nowhere. There are visions, emotions, and sometimes even premonitions involved.

This particular download came one night when I was in between sleep and wakefulness. I saw, clear as day, a series of meditations. They were written in my handwriting on this unique brown paper that looked like tree bark. There were ten of them, and each one had a focus for visualization and a connection to the outside world. I got up and wrote down everything in as much detail as I could describe.

The next morning, I started practicing these meditations. I started each one by entering a state of mindfulness, and then I transitioned to the prescribed visualization for that week. These progressed from reflecting on who I am to gratitude practice for my current self to future-self visualizations, and finally, to gratitude for my future self's accomplishments.

I went through the ten-week process, incorporating the connections to the external world, and almost immediately,

I started seeing changes. I started to process my emotions following the loss of my friends. I also realized I was gaining no internal satisfaction from all the stuff I had accumulated, and that I was confined to a space that no longer served me. I continued with my visualizations and practiced bringing mindfulness into my everyday life. I felt myself transforming. I felt my energy shifting, and I received so much clarity. All of a sudden, opportunities came knocking at my door, and decisions were made seemingly out of nowhere. My mom had always tried to talk me into moving to Europe, so she could return to Poland. All of a sudden, I started entertaining that idea.

Before I knew it, we had a flight booked to Spain to see how we'd like to live there. When we loved it and decided to pursue the idea of moving, my mom decided to move to Poland. Now alone, John and I felt free to start thinking about leaving Connecticut, but we still had our rental business established there. We said, "Let's sell one and see how it goes." It sold for $35,000 over asking! And the rest of them followed suit.

Things were just falling away, freeing us from the confines of Manchester, Connecticut. With no friends and no family holding us in place, we were free to go anywhere. We started fantasizing about taking an RV trip before moving to Spain, but we couldn't figure out how to do that with our job situations. I was working at a university at the time with my bookkeeping side hustle going, and John was a home inspector. Only one-third of our income was portable at this point.

I continued with my mindfulness practice, and I felt protective over my method, like I had just discovered something transformational, and I wanted to be the only one with access to it. I shared it with John but no one else for a while.

Then, one day, a friend was having some identity struggles. She was considering leaving her job and changing career paths completely. She did the research and knew what to do, but she was afraid to make the moves. I decided to take a leap of faith and share my manifestation method with her. Familiar with the practice of mindfulness meditation, she immediately snapped back with, "I don't see how mindfulness and manifestation can go together. They are basically opposite of one another."

I shrunk back into my shell and decided I would keep this for just myself. It worked for me, and that was all that mattered.

Something kept gnawing away at me, though. It was like there was this ball of energy growing inside of me, and it was getting uncomfortable to keep it in. I knew that Mindful Manifest Flow had to be released into the world.

I started outlining ideas for how to package up the process. I thought about coaching people face-to-face through it, because I wasn't sure how to make people understand the process in any other format. I floated the idea to another friend, who said it sounded interesting, but she doubted people would pay for it because it's "pretty common knowledge."

Ladies and gentlemen, this is why I had to leave my old life behind. I had no support for my visions. I was surrounded by people who said they loved me but did everything in their power to keep me small.

I ignored this last bit of feedback and kept going. Eventually, I landed on the idea of producing a series of guided meditation recordings, leading the listener through the same process I went through in my transformation. I got to work on this right away, trying to fit this work in among my actual work, while also taking care of the kids and helping my mom get ready for her move to Poland. I was waking up at 5:00 a.m. to plan my business. I started a new Instagram page and didn't invite any of my personal page followers to join me. I kept the whole thing a secret.

Out of nowhere, an opportunity fell in my lap. I was on a call with a client and an accountant associate of mine, and I decided to ask if he needed any help during tax season. For a while, I had been tossing around the idea of learning to prepare tax returns as an extension of my business. To my surprise, he said yes!

I started working for him soon after and found that I was picking it up quite easily. The work was flexible, on my own schedule, and I was even able to work remotely whenever I wanted. I also gained a few new bookkeeping clients.

Now I had the missing piece to my dream RV-trip puzzle. The extra bookkeeping clients added a boost to my income, and as long as I was back for the next tax season, I was free to take the trip. It's still amazing to me how quickly that plan fell into place. As soon as I decided to share Mindful Manifest Flow with the world, everything got kicked into high gear, and like a snowball rolling down a hill, my plans gained momentum and got bigger and bigger very quickly.

The RV trip gave me time to focus on myself and how I wanted the rest of my life to go. I reevaluated all of my close relationships and decided who was coming with me into the next chapter.

My journaling brought me through the very process you're working on now, the Purpose Activation Blueprint. This time around, I knew I couldn't gatekeep. I knew these downloads were coming through me, not to me. I was meant to help people transform their lives, and just like that, I knew my purpose.

I started writing this book before I even finished my process, and I made adjustments as I discovered new things. It flowed easily, and the changes I made in my life as a result of deep reflection supported my writing process. I was on the right track, and I just needed to remain consistent.

In addition to writing this book, I continued developing Mindful Manifest Flow. Before the course was ready, I started sharing on my Instagram the idea of mindful manifestation, and it slowly started gaining traction. The downloads kept coming, and before I knew it, I had my whole business trajectory outlined.

My conclusion is that the more I share of myself and my experiences and my expertise with the world, the more I receive to share. The ideas come through me, to be put into practice by me, and then to be shared. I learned that attempting to keep good things just for myself is self-centered and in direct opposition to the reason they are coming to me and not to someone else.

Mindful Manifest Flow

As of the publishing of this book, I am still working on Mindful Manifest Flow. It is coming along beautifully, but I've faced repeated delays, and it has taken longer than I thought it would. At one point, I had announced a release date and put the course up for pre-sale, but as soon as I did, everything started to fall apart, preventing me from working on the course.

First, the RV needed a repair that would take two weeks to complete, so we had to go hotel-hopping between Texas and Louisiana. Then, our Jeep needed new brakes and rotors, because my small human lodged a rock in the wheel. We got the RV back just before Christmas, and shopping needed to get done so the kids could experience the magic of a Florida Keys Christmas. (Christmas in the Keys was a bucket-list item for me, and the kids were thrilled to learn that Santa delivers to warm places, too!)

I couldn't believe how crazy this time was. One thing after another went wrong. I could barely keep up with the work that was paying the bills, so naturally, my Mindful Manifest Flow project was pushed to the back burner.

The release date I had announced to my tiny Instagram audience came and went. I had to let people know I would not be fulfilling my promise. I even had a couple of people purchase the course during the pre-sale, and I had to refund their money. Thank God they were understanding; both thanked me for being open and transparent. I promised to send them the course for free when it's ready.

When things got back on track, I found myself at a place in my writing process where I felt ready to take the next step. So, I got in touch with the publisher of this book, someone I had been following on Instagram for months, and we began our work together. Mindful Manifest Flow was pushed aside again, because I felt a tug toward this book and knew I needed to get these words out there first.

I reflected on the delays for my course, and I wondered whether I was meant to release it at all. Why would I receive this clear outline for a life-changing program that transformed my own relationship with myself and my future, if I was not meant to share it with the world? I believe I was redirected for a good reason. I decided to wait for an answer while focusing on getting this book completed.

Releasing Self-Interest

A self-centered mindset limits your perspective, causing you to focus solely on personal materialistic goals (wealth, status, power) without considering how those goals affect others. This puts you in a place of isolation and detachment from your purpose. Energy flows much better when desires serve both the individual and the collective. For example, wanting financial abundance to provide for your family and help others is more powerful than seeking money only for selfish reasons.

Letting down the wall of self-interest invites new, beautiful energy to enter into your life. When you shift your focus to serving others, you will be surprised by how quickly and how abundantly new opportunities show up at your doorstep. At that point, all you'll have to do is follow your intuition and take action.

A coaching student of mine, Lauren, worked her way through some self-serving beliefs and behaviors to achieve great success in the field of computer programming. Lauren was exceptionally gifted at coding. I couldn't tell you any more than that about her accolades, though, because her line of work is so incredibly foreign to me. I work with people and their brains, which are similar to computers in the sense that they operate based on data fed to them, but the data I feed brains is in the form of words, not zeros and ones.

In college, Lauren got an internship with a software developer, building systems that helped businesses optimize their operations. She was so advanced in her skills for her tender age of twenty-three that management offered her a full-time job before she even graduated. It was an excellent offer with high pay and great benefits. She excitedly accepted. But after a few years, the excitement faded. Despite her talent and steady paycheck, Lauren felt a sense of emptiness. She spent endless days doing the work that had once excited her to make clients she'd never met grow richer and richer. She spent years building programs that saved companies money or improved efficiency, but she felt detached and a little bored of doing the work but never seeing the impact of it.

Lauren's genius transcended the work she was doing. Without knowing anything about programming, I could tell she was not living up to her full potential. She spoke of her job as a prison for her creativity. She had ideas to increase her company's efficiency and quality of their product, but her boss was uninterested in hearing them. And because of confidentiality agreements, she never even got to see the results of her work.

In our work together, Lauren did some digging into her limiting beliefs. She uncovered that her parents really stressed how lucky she would be to get a stable and high-paying job with her degree. Her parents divorced when she was young, and both her mother and father had trouble making ends meet in single-salary households. Neither parent was highly educated.

Her father worked for several decades at a machine shop, doing physical labor, and her mother bounced around various receptionist positions. Lauren had not only watched her parents struggle financially, but she grew up hearing about the sacrifices they made for her and her brother, so they could eventually get good, high-paying jobs and never have to struggle as adults.

Lauren did love her work. She was a problem-solver and very analytical. It was the environment she was working in that was not right for her. We brainstormed ideas of where she could use her very valuable skills but also find fulfillment and purpose in her work. She told me that she liked to create apps in her spare time and had developed some software that helped her track her finances. When we started to explore the idea of launching the app to the public, Lauren met me with some resistance.

She said that her apps were far too complex for the general public, and it was not worth the time and effort to make them user-friendly. I asked her where in her work she was providing a service to others that inspires and brings her joy. When she couldn't come up with an answer, I challenged her to try being of service to others in some way, just to see how it feels. Lauren agreed to work on one of her apps to give it a simple interface.

After she streamlined the app for use by the general public, Lauren planned a small launch, not expecting much. But within weeks, the feedback poured in. She received emails and reviews from users who said the app had changed their financial lives and finally allowed them to feel in control of their money. People were gaining clarity over their finances for the first time, breaking free from debt, and saving for things that mattered to them.

Lauren's favorite review came from a fifty-five-year-old woman in Montana: "I've always been terrified of budgeting, but your app made me feel in control for the first time in my life! Now I'm planning my bucket-list trip to Iceland to see the Northern Lights, because I know how to budget and save for luxuries! Thank you, thank you, thank you."

It was the first time Lauren had felt the direct impact of her work. She wasn't just solving technical problems or making a faceless company more efficient. She was making a real difference in people's lives. And she got to witness the results! As the app grew, Lauren realized she had spent years developing her skills, but those skills had always been in service to something outside of herself and didn't drive fulfillment.

Now, for the first time, her work was directly helping others, meeting their needs in a meaningful way. It gave her a great sense of fulfillment and joy that she had never experienced before. She discovered that her purpose was realized when she combined the skills she had developed with service to others.

Eventually, Lauren left her job and started her own tech company. Now, she works hard to solve problems average people have by creating technology to address those problems. She feels fulfilled in her work and is surprised she steadily earns more money than she did at her full-time job. It turns out her lack of service to others was holding her back from realizing her full potential.

Lauren's story illustrates the creative prison many people create for themselves. It's unfortunate when you follow your passion and end up in a space not suited to your creativity and freedom. I see this all too often, where someone takes their skills and talents to an employer, and although they get to use their talents, they lack their full expression. They don't get the full benefit of serving others because they end up behind layers of the corporate structure.

Using your skills and talents is only one piece of the puzzle. As you saw in Lauren's story, it is possible to be engaged in activities that follow your purpose, but enjoyment of the work will be short-lived if you lack control over your work.

Lauren was essentially a worker-bee. Although she was doing what she loved and what she was good at, she was not fulfilled because she was not doing it the way she wanted to. When she finally unleashed her creative genius in an unapologetic, unhindered way, that's when she started living her purpose.

Purpose Evolution

You might be wondering at this point—is it possible to work a normal job and feel fulfilled? The answer is 100% yes! *But the employment conditions must be aligned to your needs and creative expression.* It may seem like I'm advocating for the quit-your-job movement, which I am, because I love entrepreneurship, but the truth is many people find purpose through their nine-to-five work.

It's not always easy, finding the right alignment between your values, talents, skills, and needs, on the one hand, and the culture and requirements of the workplace, on the other. When you find it, though, you can feel it almost immediately. Can you recall a job where it just felt like you were in the right place? Or maybe the contrary? A job where you could tell immediately that it was not the right fit for you?

I went through a lot of this when I was bartending in college and grad school. I worked at several restaurants during those years, and I became intuitive enough to know whether a job was going to work out pretty much on the first day. I've been known to work one shift and never show up again, when the vibe was wrong. Sorry, but I'm not sorry.

The key here is to pay attention to how you feel throughout your employment. A job that feels aligned at first can go south really quickly, if, for example, there is a high turnover in staff (as there often is in restaurants) or new management, new policies, etc. Unlike running your own business or being in upper-level management, when you are an employee, you are at the mercy of the employer, and the culture of the workplace is beyond your control.

The nice (and sometimes difficult) thing about purpose is that I can't tell you what qualifies as fulfilling work and what doesn't. Although I know that some level of service to others needs to be a component, it can look different for different people. For example, I found no sense of fulfillment working in auto insurance claims. I was constantly dealing with stressed-out, angry people who'd just been in a car accident, and I found myself matching their stress and anger.

I had a coworker, though, who was exceptional at leveling with people, and she found the work immensely fulfilling. I remember her gushing about how good it felt to help people through some of the most difficult times in their lives, which was a direct contradiction to the way I felt about the job. As far as I know, that woman is still working for the same company, but is now in high-level management and loves her work.

For other people, a job is just a job, and the purpose and fulfillment they fill their cups with happens outside of work. I had a coworker at the accounting firm I worked for who only worked during tax season, February to April. Although she liked the work and was good at it, she much preferred to be at home, raising her son. Her service to others was accounted for in her presence at home, taking care of her family. I do suspect, however, she'll be searching for something fulfilling to do once her son gets older and is more self-sufficient.

As you can probably see, purpose is not a one-size-fits-all concept, and there's no one way to achieve it. In my experience, most people find their purpose through their work at some point in their lives.

Purpose evolves over time because we, too, evolve as we go through different seasons in our lives. The stay-at-home mom who finds her life fulfilling as she raises her children will likely need to pivot when the kids are teenagers and don't need her as much anymore. A career-driven person may find themselves being tugged in the direction of home after they have kids. A job that was once fulfilling may begin to feel overwhelming as a new parent attempts to balance work and home life. The path changes, our needs change, and we need to be able to adapt to the many seasons of life.

The most important thing about finding purpose is to be mindful of your own well-being. Checking in to see if what you're doing still feels good is a necessary part of the process.

I like to do this in the New Year. I spend some time reflecting on the work I'm doing and analyzing how I feel about it. I then set intentions for the year ahead and outline any new ideas I have floating around. This helps to put me in the right headspace for creating and always keeps me aligned with my purpose.

In the coaching world, I know several people who have evolved their businesses over the years because what once felt like their calling now feels like a burden. Others have changed their service offerings to make more money and later found out they no longer love their work. Often, they go back to making less money but serving people in a more aligned way. The evolution of purpose is certainly not linear.

Chapter 8 Exploration Exercises

The following reflective activities are meant to get you thinking about how you can find purpose in serving others. By this point, you may already have an idea of what your purpose is. Completing these reflections will hopefully help you solidify the ways in which you can act on your purpose in a satisfying and fulfilling way.

1. Recognize Your Unique Contribution

Go back to your Skills and Strengths Inventory from Chapter 4. Brainstorm ways you can use each one in service to others, whether in your personal life, work, or community. Reflect on which strengths bring you the most fulfillment when using them to help others.

2. Visualize Your Ideal Legacy

Write a "legacy letter" to your future self, describing how you hope to be remembered for the ways you served others. Outline the kind of impact you want to have and how it aligns with your purpose. This can help clarify what aspects of service are most important to you moving forward. Consider:

- What impact would you like to have made on the lives of others? This can be your family or a community of people.
- How would you want people to remember you in terms of service and contribution?

3. **Explore Barriers to Service**

Reflect on one or two specific barriers that may be preventing you from giving back or helping others. Identify the limiting beliefs or fears behind these barriers, and brainstorm ways to overcome them. (We'll revisit this in the next chapter.)

Consider how removing these obstacles could deepen your sense of purpose and connection with others.

CHAPTER 9

Overcoming Fear and Doubt

NOW THAT YOU'VE ASSEMBLED the pieces of your Purpose Activation Blueprint, let's explore some things that might hold you back from fulfilling your purpose. It's important to acknowledge the fear that might hold you back before formulating your purpose statement, because, otherwise, you might miss some important clues due to unconscious fears and doubts. If you've identified them upfront, you are much better suited to completing your analysis through a more objective lens, rather than operating from a place of emotion.

Let me preface this chapter by giving you a warning that it's long, and I don't have a concrete solution to offer for eliminating fears. I've spent more time on this chapter than any other in the book, because I believe the secret to living a life of freedom and fulfillment is learning to overcome fears.

Notice I did not say *eliminate* fears, because that is not possible. Rather, we learn to identify fears, get to know them, and then move through them. And the more you do this, the easier it becomes, because you begin to see the rewards of pushing through. It becomes addicting in a way, and you begin to feel like you can conquer anything, despite the fear you will inevitably feel. Fear becomes a companion in your journey to your ideal reality, not a deterrent.

The True Nature of Fear

Fear is a strong emotion. It's what keeps us in place. And unfortunately, our fears can be played upon by those who wish us to stay put. Fear can be used as a manipulative tactic by people who love us as a way to spare our feelings of failure. It can be used by those close to us who do not have the best intention. And it can be used on a much broader scale by systems that benefit from us staying small and scared.

Let's dive into each of these in some detail, so you can begin to understand that fear, the way it is meant to be felt and what it is meant to do biologically, has been hijacked by modern society.

The true nature of fear, the one that is supposed to help us to survive and reproduce (which is the whole entire purpose of life, according to evolutionary psychology), is that we are supposed to be afraid of things that can harm us physically and hence can be detrimental to our survival. Instinctually, we are supposed to be fearful of predators, injury, loss of resources, and social rejection.

In our modern society, we are relatively protected from predators and loss of resources. Our fears of heights, falling, fire, drowning, germs, etc., take care of the injury and illness piece. That just leaves social rejection as the only basic fear we're left with.

Social rejection was a useful fear for our ancient ancestors because staying in groups provided more safety and protection, which increased the chances of survival and reproduction. According to evolution theory, the humans who were more social and cared more about being accepted within the group lived longer and were able to pass down their genes of social coexistence over those who were ostracized from the group, either by choice or by consequence. This is how we evolved to care what others think.

Nowadays, we don't have to worry as much about being eaten by a predator as we did thousands of years ago, and we get our meat and berries from a grocery store instead of hunting and gathering them. Within the last hundred years or so, we've made survival almost a sure thing through modern medicine and social welfare programs. No longer do we have to wonder if we're going to die from an infected paper cut, and we've put systems in place to help those who fall upon hard times. Comparatively, life is pretty easy.

Our minds are equipped with a standard fear option, though. So, where do we place our fears, now that we can live without worry for our general safety and survival? On social matters, of course!

We've evolved an immensely distinct social compass, where all we want to do is fit in and belong. This desire was once useful because, in ancient times, you would have been cast out of the group if you didn't fit in, and your survival would have been in jeopardy, but today, you're not going to die if Becky doesn't like you.

But we feel this social pressure greatly! "If Becky doesn't like me, she's going to talk about me to our mutual friends, and then they won't like me, and I won't have friends anymore, and I'll never meet the love of my life, because I'll have to sit home all day without friends to go out with, and I'll just die alone."

Maybe not specifically that thought sequence, but have you ever gone down a rabbit hole like this? Where irrational thoughts spiral to a doomsday conclusion not at all based in reality? Or how about the increase in depression and anxiety in our culture? This is a prime example of the misuse of our old survival systems. In the ancient days of our evolution, anxiety would have helped us to remain alert and avoid danger, while depression may have encouraged withdrawal from social interaction and allowed for rest during stressful times, which could have helped us stay protected.

In modern times, anxiety and depression are worldwide epidemics, consuming millions of people each day. For the vast majority of people suffering from these debilitating illnesses, it's not because they are fighting for their physical safety; it's because of social pressures. And instead of increasing our chances of survival, they actually threaten to take our lives.

Fears and Purpose

You might be wondering how this all relates to our discussion of purpose. It's because there are millions of people not pursuing their purpose due to fear. Many people are called to do something in life, which they have identified and they understand the assignment very well, but they take no action toward it because fear and doubt take hold of them.

I worked with a thirty-something-year-old named Christina, who had a clear vision of what her purpose was. Ever since she was young, she'd had a gift for helping people navigate life's challenges. She could listen, provide comfort, and guide them to find the silver lining in the challenges they faced. Friends would always confide in her, and even adults found themselves spilling their problems to her when she was a teenager. Christina's dream had always been to become a life coach, empowering others to find their purpose and live fulfilling lives. But life had a way of clouding that dream.

I met Christina through social media. She resonated with my story because she craved a life and business rooted in freedom, much like what I was sharing from my own life on my platforms. We had many parallels in our stories, and she wanted to learn how to transition to fulfilling work.

Christina had two small children, ages three and five, who were her world. She also had a stable management-level job in corporate marketing that provided financial security for her family. She was successful and lived a happy life, yet something gnawed at her. She felt a sense that she was living a life not aligned with her true calling.

Every day on her commute to work, Christina would imagine what it might be like to start her own coaching business. Then, the familiar wave of fear would rush in. "What if I fail? What if I can't provide for my kids? What if I'm not good enough? What will my parents think? What will people say?" Doubt reared its ugly head, paralyzing her.

Her corporate job was safe. It paid the bills and allowed her to take care of her children. But her intense schedule and unpredictable deadlines were not conducive to starting a side hustle. She needed to be all in or all out. Leaving her job behind felt reckless, but the thought of staying made her feel like she was suffocating.

When we started our work together, she disclosed that her husband didn't know she'd signed on to work with me. She connected with my story on Instagram immediately, and, on a whim, she booked a coaching call with me. She said, "Teach me everything you did to get to where you are. I want step-by-step directions to start my own coaching business."

I laughed because this is how I think, too. I want detailed instructions for everything, and I expect my results to be exactly the same as the person providing the instructions. Unfortunately, life doesn't work that way. I told her, "You don't want to follow my lead. What I did led to selling everything I owned, leaving everything I've ever known behind, and living in an RV. It's not for the faint of heart!" She agreed that it was the business I had built that she desired, not my gypsy lifestyle.

When we really got the core of her fears, Christina discovered that they were all rooted in social pressures. I asked her what would happen if she quit her job and went all in on starting a coaching business. Our conversation went something like this:

C: I might fail! And then I won't have my job to fall back on.

Me: And then what would happen?

C: We wouldn't have enough money to pay our bills. What if we lose the house?

Me: What would happen if you lost the house? Could you downsize?

C: Yes, we could definitely downsize, and we could live off my husband's salary in a smaller house with older cars, but then what would people think? They would blame me for putting my family's welfare at risk for my silly hobby of talking to people!

It only took *two* follow up questions to get to the core of Christina's problem. She couldn't even get past the "what would people think?" spiral to share with her husband what her dream was. As far as he knew, Christina was living her dream life, happy as a clam.

We ran some more "and then what would happen?" scenarios, until Christina came to the conclusion that she could, without a shadow of a doubt, afford to take this risk. Yes, some sacrifices would be required, and her husband would need to be onboard with the plan, but when she got rid of her worry about what people would think, she got started on making the moves to start living her purpose.

Lo and behold, her husband was 100% supportive, and they went to work right away on her plan. They downgraded their expensive cars, entered a buy-nothing period, took their kids out of daycare, and stopped spending money on dining and entertainment. This easily got them through the transition period, and Christina landed her first coaching client within two months of starting her business. It just snowballed from there, and now she makes more money in her coaching business than she did in her marketing job.

When we really dissect our fears, it's not surprising to find that there are social pressures at the core of them. "What will people think?" is only one of them. We also have "What if I fail?", "What if I'm not good enough?" and (my favorite), "What will change if I succeed?" Let's dive into each of these in some more detail.

Fear of Failure

By far, the fear of failure is the most common reason for avoiding fulfillment. In ancient times, if we failed at something, it often meant we died. Failing to find food or shelter or failing to protect ourselves from predators resulted in deadly consequences. In modern times, failure is not quite so life-threatening, but our brains are wired to operate as if it is.

Of course, the good old "what will people think?" fear comes into play. We try so hard to maintain a certain public image that we strategically avoid taking risks that could result in public failure. When I was taking my various licensing exams throughout my career arc, I didn't tell a single soul until I actually passed, because I didn't want the "How did you do?" and the follow-up "Aww, it's okay, you'll pass next time" spiel if I failed.

I also believe that energy transfers, and if someone secretly hopes you'll fail, it can affect your outcome. As I've shared earlier, I didn't get much support for my dreams from the people close to me. As a result, I much prefer to make my moves in silence.

So, why does it feel so defeating to fail in public? Well, for starters, society puts an incredible emphasis on perfectionism. In the media, we only see stories of people who have already achieved success. For example, on the real estate TV shows, we only see the agents and brokers who are making millions of dollars. There are no shows about agents just starting out, spending their weekends passing out business cards at the open houses of the more successful agents in their office, attending every networking event under the sun, and getting offended when a family member or a friend hires a more experienced agent to sell their house. (How do I know this so specifically? I've done it!) We only get to see the shiny, impressive parts of success in the media.

That's the media's fault. If you're looking to shift the blame inward, however, consider any time you heard about someone you know starting a new business. Did you judge them? Did you assume they would fail? Did you even pay attention? We tend to not support one another when it involves something out of the norm.

I can't tell you how many people assume my success came overnight, when, in reality, I was working on it all along but no one cared to pay attention. It's the end result that grabs attention, once the person has already overcome the challenges they inevitably faced. We tend to ignore the process. From the outside, it looks like they became an overnight success and skyrocketed to their new level. If we watched the whole process of someone's success from the start, however, it might feel less overwhelming and more relatable.

When you really stop to think about how much pressure there is to succeed, it's no wonder we fear failure. The desire for perfection is so deep-rooted, in fact, that most people tie it to their self-worth. For many, failure equals a personal, irreversible flaw. But in reality, that's not at all how failure works! Failure is a learning opportunity and a chance to try again in a different way.

If you're one of the many who think like this, only feeling confident when you're successful, I've got news for you. You have *conditional* self-worth. You're probably someone who over-gives, overworks, and overdoes everything you touch. You might play things over and over in your head, analyzing everything that went wrong, and beating yourself up for it. You lack self-compassion.

If this sounds like you, you probably have a massive fear of failure. You prefer to stay small and relatively successful rather than try something new and not being perfect at it, especially if it involves a public image. I say all of this with absolute love and compassion, because I was you.

I was terrified of putting myself out there and being judged or laughed at. When I first realized my purpose in life requires me to present myself publicly, I almost stayed put in my tax work. The number of times I said to myself, "This is never going to work," has probably broken some world records.

Ironically, I started my business on Instagram, the most public way to fail. To be honest, I wasn't sure where to start, and at first, I had a completely different plan. But I saw how digital creators were reaching tons of people on Instagram, and I had a lot to share, so I jumped on.

At first, it was clunky. I knew what I wanted to share, but I didn't know how to share it. My content was getting low views, I had a small following, and I worried about what people I knew were going to say. I envisioned my family in Poland coming across my content and thinking, "What the hell is she doing?" I also worried about people from my past seeing what I was doing. At least half of them would be laughing at me, thinking I was going to fail, and the other half would be genuinely concerned, wondering if I'd lost my mind.

I was throwing around the word *manifestation* and instructing people to believe in themselves, when I didn't really fully believe in myself. It was the energy of that disconnect that impeded my success. My constant self-doubt interfered with my consistency, and comparing my content to those who were successful was killing my confidence.

I came across a coach who was advertising to women with a fear of being seen. I had never heard it quite put that way, and I was intrigued because that's exactly how I felt! I listened to some of her content, and I booked a call with her.

This was so out of my norm that, when she said the coaching package cost $3,000, I almost spit out my tea. Although this price tag is a drop in the bucket compared to other coaching programs that I've spent money on since then, it was quite a shock to me at the very beginning on this journey. People really do spend *a lot* of money on personal development, and for good reason!

I thanked her for her time and concluded I was just going to give up. This was not for me.

When I told my husband about it, however, he surprised me by saying, "Do you think it'll help?"

I said I wasn't sure, but it seemed like this woman knew my issues, and she claimed she could help resolve them. I knew it was my energy and my hesitation that was holding me back. John reminded me we were cashing out of a property soon and we would have an influx of money coming in. We decided we were in a comfortable-enough place that we could give it a try.

In this group coaching program, I was introduced to techniques for energetic work and subconscious reprogramming. We did a lot of EFT (Emotional Freedom Techniques) tapping, visualization, journaling, and affirmations around the fear of being seen. The work helped me to see how irrational the fear of being seen really is. I was able to step into a new mindset of "who cares what they think?" because, at the end of the day, the cost of not pursuing your dreams is much more costly than the social rejection you might face.

When I started to embody this new way of thinking, I started seeing a change in my consistency. I was determined to keep trying, keep failing, and keep learning.

I read a quote that said, "How would you show up differently if you knew you were only thirty more failures away from success?" This resonated with me because, while failing thirty times is a lot, knowing that success is just a matter of ticking off the failures moved me to show up differently. I wanted to get those failures over with as quickly as possible. So, I decided that I *wanted* to fail.

I began to wear failure as a badge of honor, because I was proud of myself for trying and it was feedback for my processes that I could use to become better. I analyzed what worked and what didn't, and I continued learning. I came up with a strategy and a plan that worked for my life without becoming too burdensome.

Then, something clicked. In the midst of my podcast listening, masterclass watching, and doing the comment-a-word-for-a-guide exercises, I realized what was missing. I had a vision of who I wanted to be and what I wanted to do. But I wasn't that person yet. I learned that I had to embody not only the mindset of who I was becoming, but also the behaviors and habits of that person.

When I asked myself what the successful version of me does and, even more importantly, doesn't do, I realized I needed to stop drinking, prioritize my sleep, work on my business dedicatedly and consistently, and carry myself like I'm worth the millions of dollars I desired to make. When I started doing this, all of the fears and doubts melted away. The energy shift I experienced changed everything for me.

How to Embody Your Higher Self

What I'm about to say right here is the most valuable part of this book. This advice can change your life, as it did mine. I'm going to articulate here for you the methods I use in my own spiritual practice, which I also apply with my clients.

This advice, in my opinion, is the best-kept secret of successful people.

Here it is: to become the higher version of yourself, you have to become the higher version of yourself. I know, I know. Those are the same words repeated, but hear me out. Let me try to break this down.

The desires you have and the life you want to live are not random or common to everyone. You might think, "Well surely everyone desires to live the life I want to live," but in reality, your dreams are not the dreams of everyone else. Sure, most people want success, nice cars, big houses, fancy clothes, etc., but the *life* you desire and the means to get you the fancy things are unique to you.

Let me give you an example. When I first started on my work, I used to think everyone wanted to write a book, speak on stages, and host transformational events. I mean, why wouldn't they? It sounds so fulfilling and empowering to make a name for yourself in this way!

But when I described my ambitions to a friend at one point, she said, "Ugh, I'd rather die than speak on a stage. That sounds horrible." I asked her what would be fulfilling to her, and she said her goal in life is to start a supportive voluntary group home for folks affected by loss, grief, and mental health struggles. I thought that was noble, but I sure as hell would not want to do that.

I realized in that moment we're so one-track minded and absorbed in our own worlds, it's difficult to see beyond our own thoughts and beliefs. Toddlers think like this before they develop something called *theory of mind*. They can't understand that another person's perspective could be different from their own.

Just like toddlers, we often assume everyone thinks like us. The things we want are so logical to *us*, we think everyone else wants them, too. This couldn't be further from the truth.

Your vision is uniquely yours. Other people don't want what you want, and you're being called to it because you have something within you that makes you suited for it. Just like people are attracted to one another by some invisible force called love, we are attracted to certain things because of an invisible force called purpose.

Hopefully, I've convinced you that the life you desire is meant for you. Next, you have to start acting like it. The only way to get everything you desire is to behave as if it's already yours. No doubts, no worries, no fears, just embodying this higher version of yourself and trusting that the actions you are taking are bringing you closer to that reality.

This involves shifting your mindset to believing in yourself and your calling. Believe that you deserve the life you want and you are worthy of it. When you do, opportunities will begin to appear that will bring you closer to the life you desire. Your job is to take the opportunities without overthinking it.

The act of truly and trustingly embodying your higher self is called *quantum leaping*. Now, please understand, this is heavy work. It's a process of changing who you are at a fundamental level. It cannot be accomplished overnight, and most people require some level of coaching to learn how to do this effectively. Of course, in this format, I can only tell you what needs to be done and not *how* to do it, because the *how* looks different for each person.

I will end this extremely valuable lesson with this: You are meant for your purpose. The life you want begins the moment you stop doubting yourself. When you become the higher version of yourself, you will become the higher version of yourself.

Fear of What Others Will Think

If you're a people-pleaser, your biggest fear might be disappointing others. I almost accidentally left this part out because I'm a people-agitator and I forget that millions are afflicted by the people-pleasing virus. This is an area of self-help where I struggle to teach with compassion. My go-to resolution is always, "Fuck what they think, and do what makes you happy," but that's not great advice for someone who literally drowns in others' opinions and can't breathe without social acceptance.

Although I was never what I would call a "people-pleaser," I was definitely held back by what others thought of me for a while, so I have experienced the fear of what others will think, too.

We've already discussed the immense pressure we feel to be socially accepted, so it's no wonder that there are millions, maybe billions of people out there who are crippled by their fear of disappointing people. It keeps them stuck in place, doing the socially acceptable things that are expected of them, even if this contradicts their morals and beliefs, or even if it feels like they're dying inside by not living up to their full potential.

This pressure can come from parents, peers, or society in general. Often, a path is laid out for our life and happiness long before we have the opportunity to make decisions for ourselves. Parents have certain expectations of who we'll be, peers expect us to fit in with their standards of "normal," and society has prescribed us a list of accomplishments, accompanied by the age by which they must be fulfilled. It's no wonder doing your own thing is hard—everyone around you is telling you you're doing it wrong.

Some people are better at letting opinions and expectations roll off than others. There's a multitude of reasons for this, including both innate and environmental factors, or *nature and nurture*. It is generally accepted that part of our personality is genetically inherited and part of it is conditioned by our upbringing and environment.

The best evidence for inherited personality traits is the concept of temperament, which we went over briefly in Chapter 7. Temperament is considered the precursor to personality, and it's something babies are born with. Some babies are generally easy, happy, and calm, while others are sensitive, tend to be difficult, and experience intense emotions, and still others are shy at first and then warm up, as they feel more comfortable. There are a good number of babies who end up being a mix of two or three of these styles.

Research has shown that these temperament styles are good predictors of certain personality traits in adulthood. For example, the easy babies tend to grow up into emotionally stable adults with good social skills and solid confidence. The difficult babies grow up to be more assertive, creative, and passionate. And the slow-to-warm-up babies will be thoughtful and reserved.

While temperament style is a good predictor of adulthood personality, it's not the whole picture. Environment and experience shape who we are, too, and the way the temperament style is responded to by caregivers is also a factor. For example, if the difficult-temperament child is raised in an environment where their assertiveness is suppressed and punished, they might either seek out approval from others or rebel when they grow up, whereas a child whose assertiveness is encouraged will likely grow up to be an assertive adult who will prioritize their own happiness and not give a damn what others think.

Without resistance from their environment, the difficult babies are the least likely to develop people-pleasing habits, while the slow to warm up babies are the most likely, and the easy babies are also relatively likely. This means *most* people are predisposed to develop people-pleasing habits. So, if you fall into this category, you're in good company. (And yes, I was a difficult baby. Sorry, Mom!)

Great. Now we know why you are the way you are. But how do you overcome your fear of what others think? Well, the first step in overcoming any fear is being able to acknowledge it and getting comfortable with it. Fear is not actually something we eliminate. It's something we push through, despite the internal resistance we feel.

Fears will always exist in one way or another. We are programmed this way, and it's not something we can get rid of entirely. Instead, we can reprogram our fears to be less scary and debilitating. We can work with our fears and get to know them. This way, we feel empowered to do the thing, despite the fear. And the more you do that, the easier it becomes for subsequent decisions that require pushing through the fear.

Let's talk about this in a practical way in relation to people-pleasing.

Understanding why you have the habit. I did my due diligence in explaining this from a broad, scientific level, but each specific case of people-pleasing is nuanced, and your life experience largely determines both the extent of the people-pleasing tendencies and how much it truly holds you back.

It's helpful to do some journaling on the topic to reflect on what in your past has reinforced these tendencies. If you do the reflection and truly come up with nothing, you can probably chalk it up to genetics. But I would venture to guess that there is at least some component of conditioning involved in your habit.

Challenge the fear. Begin to reflect on times in your past where people in your life disagreed with or judged something you chose to do and what the outcomes were. Try to be rational about the outcomes and where the choice led you. Often, our perception of consequences is much worse than what really happened. We tend to get carried away with our recollection of some situations that don't put us in a good light.

It might be uncomfortable to revisit those old wounds, but it's important to see the progress beyond the conflict. You might be surprised to see just what resulted from disappointing people and following your own instincts. I'd be willing to bet some good things came about.

Reprogram the fear. Change your limiting beliefs from, "They won't like me if I say no to this," to "I'm not defined by what they think." You can do this by using affirmations, EFT Tapping, journaling from the perspective of your future self, or visualizing yourself disappointing others with positive outcomes for yourself. Feeding this new data to your subconscious will help you move through the fear.

Move with the fear. If your subconscious is trying to convince you that all hell will break loose when you do something that actually honors your own will because others will be disappointed, thank your subconscious for the input, and then do the thing anyway. Easier said than done, but the only way to overcome fear is to push through it.

Your subconscious will pipe up every step of the way, and it will try to stop you. Keep acknowledging its input, and keep moving. The more you do this, the more you'll get used to the discomfort, and it won't deter you anymore. Once you're comfortable being uncomfortable, you will be unstoppable.

Fear of Not Being Enough

The fears of failure and of what others will think are pressures that come from our external world. On the other hand, the fear of not being enough is a pressure from our own internal view. This one sneaks up on you without much warning and is less obvious than the other two.

When we're embarking on something big, especially if it's something we've never done before, we approach it as a novice. I mean, everyone needs to start somewhere. And when we're new at something, we tend to lack confidence. Even if you approach a new venture from a place of education and solid preparation, confidence still takes a while to build. Please note, *this is normal*. You can get all the training your heart desires, practice your new skill with supervision, study the theory behind what you're doing until you pass out, and you will still feel like you don't know what you're doing when the time comes to go out on your own or charge for your services.

There are a few reasons for this. The first is that studying theory, while important to grasping the fundamentals of a new skill, does not translate to actual skill. People know a whole lot about things they cannot themselves actually perform.

For example, when I was getting licensed as a realtor, the course I took was all about rules and ethics and nothing about how to work with people and be a salesperson. I learned a lot about easements, and I aced the exam, but I sucked at selling real estate. I could teach that class right now, but put me in a room with an eager seller and a ready buyer, and I'll just facilitate the conversation rather than take charge of it.

I never developed the "sales skill." This is because, at my core, I am someone who reflects rather than steers. My strength lies in helping people understand themselves, and we'd end up with a buyer and a seller who each understand *why* they want the deal they're looking for, but no deal will be made.

If I had really committed to developing my sales skills, maybe I'd be much better at it by now. I realized early on, however, that I felt inauthentic in that role and my confidence was in the tank. I didn't like sugar-coating things that did not sit right with me, and I really did not like what it took to market myself, like cold calling (yes, we called strangers on the phone back in the day—cringe) and hosting open houses for other agents.

In most industries, confidence comes with practice, by actually doing the job. So, first and foremost, you have to like the work you're doing to gain the skills. But even if you do like it and have been working for several years, you might still doubt your skills. Why is this? It's called *imposter syndrome*.

Imposter syndrome happens when we doubt our abilities and achievements. We feel like a fraud, even though we're actually really successful and good at what we're doing. The fear of not being enough rears its ugly head, and we worry we'll be exposed as incapable or underskilled.

Imposter syndrome can look different depending on where the fear is coming from. For example, someone who sets really high standards and tends to be a perfectionist might doubt their abilities when they make a mistake or when something doesn't quite go as planned. (Hi, I'm Izabela, and I'm a perfectionist.)

We can be really hard on ourselves when something goes wrong and start to wonder if we're cut out for what we're doing. I went through a lot of this in my bookkeeping business. I would cycle through thoughts of, "I'm so good at this," and "I have no idea what I'm doing," depending on how smoothly my work was going. Sometimes, both thoughts could exist in the very same day! Everyone makes mistakes, and every industry requires constant learning. The truth is I *was* good at it. All I had to do was look at the money people were willing to pay me for my skills and the fact that my clients stuck by me for many years as confirmation.

Another sign of imposter syndrome is overpreparing. We see this in someone who will take course after course, constantly learning about the thing they are trying to do, but will never feel prepared enough. This leads to avoidance of what needs to be done to succeed. You might avoid taking on new roles, turn down opportunities for growth, or keep yourself small, so you can stay comfortable in your little bubble.

In reality, you need to just do the thing in order to really get good at it. Success is built outside of your comfort zone. Courses and training provide you with background knowledge and some skills, but there is no scenario where you will learn each and every thing you will need in your work before you start actually doing the work.

A few more signs can include discounting your success, feeling out of place, and comparing yourself to others. All of these will have you doubting yourself and playing small so that your subconscious can avoid feeling not good enough.

Imposter syndrome can be overcome by simply shifting your mindset. Reframing mistakes as opportunities for growth can help your subconscious shift its perspective so it will no longer fear trying new things to avoid failure.

Here are some suggestions for making this mindset shift (and any mindset shift, for that matter):

Journaling on your doubts and fears. When limiting beliefs pop up, try to write about them.

- First, identify what happened that made you feel like you're not enough. For example, making a mistake, getting a negative comment, struggling to come up with an answer right away, etc.
- Next, write out the thought process that followed the feeling of not enough. Maybe you started

doubting your skills, comparing yourself to others, or felt out of place.

- Finally, rewrite the thing that happened to make you feel this way, but follow it with reframed thoughts. For example, "I made a mistake, but I owned it, I learned from it, and I will not make the same mistake again." Or, "I appreciate all feedback, positive and negative. If it's constructive, I will use it to get better, and if it's not constructive, I will ignore it."

Identifying the doubts and fears brings you eighty percent of the way to reprogramming them. Use that momentum, and flip them to make your limiting beliefs activated by fear or doubt a positive learning experience.

Visualizing failure: This might seem counterintuitive, but I invite you to sit down and visualize your fear coming true. The worst thing you're afraid will happen, that's the one I want you to take head on.

- Visualize it happening, and then visualize yourself overcoming it. For example, if you're triggered by negative feedback from others, imagine yourself getting a nasty comment or review.
- Allow yourself to feel the frustration of this, and then see yourself overcoming it.
- Imagine what you would do in response, what you would say to the person or to the public, and what you would tell yourself.

If you get carried away and any of your visualized responses are negative or retaliatory, try again. The goal is to get to a point where you react with positivity and grace, not allowing the setback to define you and your abilities.

Taking a third-person approach: Imagine your friend came to you with the fear or doubt you're experiencing. Think about what you would say to them, what you would recommend, and how you would encourage them to keep going despite the doubt. It's amazing how good we are at giving others advice and how bad we are at giving ourselves the same advice.

You have the knowledge and the encouragement within you already. You just need to direct it inward.

Fear of What Will Change

The fear of what will change is one that we're often not conscious of. We can pinpoint and make some sense of fear of failure, people pleasing, and fear of not being enough, but with fear of what will change, it can be hard to reconcile your resistance. I mean, the point of this spiritual and introspective journey is to change, isn't it? So, why would we fear change?

It's not so much the actual change we fear. The change is what we want and what we strive for, but it's the "what else in my life is going to change with it?" that we fear.

We've already touched on a few of the things you will not be able to bring with you into your new, fulfilled life: friends and family who hold you back, old beliefs, and material possessions that do not fit your new outlook on life. We can add to this list: predictability and control.

As you can imagine, stepping *into* your purpose will require you to step *out* of your comfort zone. You will need to try new things that better align with the person you are becoming. It will feel uncomfortable at first, and your subconscious will try to tell you that you can't do it, so you'll return to your comfort zone. (Remember, the subconscious hates feeling uncomfortable.) But you must push through those feelings.

When you do, things will feel different. You'll begin to see your own bullshit excuses that kept you small, and you'll start to pick out the people who are not meant to move forward with you. Once on the other side of the work, the old excuses you identify that held you back will make you shake your head at how you've limited yourself. But old beliefs die hard. Even when you consciously identify the beliefs that have held you back, they will creep in here and there.

If you can recall from Chapter 6, the subconscious operates on data. It forms its beliefs based on experiences you've had and things you've learned along the way. Some beliefs run super-deep, formed on tons and tons of data confirming the belief. Scarcity is one such belief. This one is exceptionally strong because our society operates on it. The data confirming scarcity does not just come from our own experiences; it is taught by our parents and reinforced by society.

If you'd like proof of this, just watch the news for ten minutes. I can almost guarantee there will be a mention of "not enough." Either eggs are too expensive, toilet paper is running out in stores (remember this during the pandemic? Wild times.), or there's not enough housing to go around. This is media fear-mongering at its finest.

Society benefits from our collective scarcity mindset, because it leads to consumerism. When we fear not having enough, we are driven to seek more. Enter: The Toilet Paper

Hoarding Era of 2020. Personally, I went beyond toilet paper and started hoarding everything from dish soap to sandwich bags, because "you never know what might happen with the supply chain." My basement was stacked with extra stuff, all of which got donated when I sold my house. And to this day, the world has not run out of sandwich bags.

So, how do we reprogram such a deeply ingrained, strongly emphasized limiting belief? The only possible way: with data to the contrary. The first step is to turn off the news. The less scarcity-supporting data you expose your subconscious to, the better. Step two is to look for data that supports abundance and really take it in. We tend to ignore information that contradicts our belief system (as mentioned, this is called *confirmation bias*), and we take particular notice of things out of the ordinary.

For example, typically, you wouldn't pay attention to a fully-stocked grocery store, because that's how it's supposed to be. But slap a *Limit 3 dozen eggs per customer* sign on the fridge door, and people lose their minds, further reinforcing the scarcity mindset. But take a moment to look around at the store. Everything else is fully stocked. Can you maybe eat something else for breakfast in the short term? Or maybe three dozen will suffice for the week, if you can afford the higher cost?

This simple mindset shift protects you from digging even deeper into the scarcity belief. It provides support to the contrary—that there is actually abundance. And thus, slowly but surely, the subconscious mind begins to shift your limiting beliefs as you do this more and more.

The people you can't take with you into your new life will be a harder pill to swallow. Letting go of limiting beliefs feels good, but letting go of people does not. We build strong connections over time, and it's hard to imagine life without certain people. If I told you that your best friend, the one you have decades of memories with, the one you can be yourself around and speak to more freely than anyone else in your life, is not suitable for your new life, and in order to become the best version of you, you have to let them go, would you hesitate making the changes to better your life? What if I told you that it's your partner who's holding you back? Would you sacrifice the progress you know you're capable of to stay behind and nurture those relationships?

I sure hope not. But if you do, please know it is very likely that those relationships will eventually fall apart anyway, because they were made for a season of your life, not the whole of it. People come into your life for different reasons, but they all leave for the same reason: they are not aligned with your future self. They can't grow with you, and tensions will arise when you begin to exit their vibrational frequency.

I had a best friend in high school and college who is no longer in my life today. I remember her fondly, as we did share a lot of experiences during our coming of age. We were both free spirits who loved to ponder the meaning of life and were known to stay up all night, talking about our wild theories of the Universe. Unfortunately, though, we grew apart. As often happens with coming-of-age friendships, we went in different directions in life. She went into the arts, and I went into the sciences. She embraced and doubled down on her abstract thinking and carefree lifestyle, while I wanted to settle down and make money.

Toward the end of the friendship, we had a falling out. She blamed the man I was with for the change in me. It was not his fault, of course. It was just the natural trajectory of my life. I wanted to get married (after years of saying I didn't), and I wanted a family. She kept trying to convince me that he was not the one for me. It wasn't a malicious intention. There were facts to support her concern, as John and I had a rough start to our relationship. But eventually, she gave me an ultimatum: it was her or him. And I did the unthinkable. I chose the guy over my best friend.

I went on to marry that guy, and we have a beautiful life together. I want to say it wasn't an easy decision to choose between them, but it actually was. Without hesitation, I chose John. It was a gut feeling, and I honored it wholeheartedly.

That's the thing with relationships not aligned with your future self—you can just *feel* they're not meant for you any longer. However, your comfort-loving subconscious will try to remind you of all the good times you've had together and all you've been through, as a way to keep you in your safe zone. So, even when all the facts point to "this is not meant for you," you will contemplate staying.

If you can recall from earlier in this book, I mentioned my friend group from which I became excluded. While I will not go into great detail about what happened (that's for the next book!), I will reiterate the trajectory of the relationship to make my point here.

When I saw that the friendships were not going to grow with me, I tried to water myself down so I could stay with them. My high school friend and I grew apart. We both grew, but in separate directions, which was a little bit easier to digest. This time around, however, the problem was that my friends did not want to grow.

Ever the entrepreneur, I was always working on something new, looking for new ideas, and expanding my businesses. I tried to bring my friends along for the ride by encouraging them to start their own businesses when they complained about their jobs, and I invited them to collaborate on projects I was working on. This was always met with resistance, and since they clearly were not interested in making any changes, my conclusion to the conversation was always, "So, stop complaining then!"

Looking back, I realize how different my mindset was from theirs. When I had something in my life I didn't like, I did something about it. I understand now that there are people who just want to complain and endure. They want to wallow in their angst and commiserate with others who also want to sit around and complain.

Eventually, I stopped pushing. I realized they were not going to change, and I could feel we were growing apart. But my life was entangled in a whole web of people at this point, each one connected to another, so if one friendship fell apart, it would cause ripples in the whole web, and I knew things would change forever.

So, I tried to hold on. I started to downplay my success and avoided talking about what I was doing in my work and new projects I was considering. No one asked me to do this, but my subconscious said, "If you want to keep your friends, stop bragging." I read a quote that said, "When you're around people who aren't growing, your growth looks like arrogance." I couldn't agree more.

When the drama died down, I also realized I changed the way I spoke when I was with them. I had gotten comments about the words I used that made me feel self-conscious. I remember someone saying once, "Okay, Izzy, we get it. You're smart. You don't have to use such big words." They also mockingly called me "Professor Izzy." Over the years, I simplified my vocabulary to avoid comments like this, and I never talked about my work (where I actually was a professor!). Imagine adults making fun of another adult for being too smart! This seriously brought me back to my childhood and made me shrink who I was, so I could fit in.

Despite my efforts, the relationships fell apart anyway. You cannot keep what is not meant for you. Silly, meaningless fights happened that snowballed into big issues. Our spouses were also all interconnected in this web, so they were affected, too. It turned into a whole big mess, and at some point, there was no turning back.

So, I did the only thing I could do—I let go. I stopped responding, I stopped engaging, and I stopped caring. The last bit was definitely the hardest for me. How do you stop caring about people you have so much history with? How do you let go of people you still love?

Not easily, I'll tell you that much. But you have to put your own well-being first and foremost. Friendships and romantic relationships are not supposed to be hard. They're not supposed to make you feel bad about yourself or watered down or like you have to put up a front to fit in. You'll know you're entwined in a bad relationship if you are not being your authentic self.

The fear of what will change can keep you stuck in an unbeneficial relationship for a long time. The sooner you get out, though, the sooner you can begin to heal. If you know it's detrimental and you know it cannot be fixed without changing who you are, I have news for you: it's not going to improve. I do say this with a grain of salt, however, because I'm a true believer in the idea that people can change. My rocky relationship with John changed dramatically over the years, and I'm truly happy I stayed with him, even when all signs pointed to: Get out.

The reason I stayed is that my intuition told me to. I'm a Human Design Generator (if you don't know your Human Design type yet, I highly suggest looking into it), and my intuition is second to none. I can literally ask it anything, and I'll know the answer that is right for me. Anyone can develop their intuition, and maybe I'll teach on this topic someday.

Ultimately, only you can decide when you've had enough. When you do decide to leave an unproductive relationship, I have a few bits of advice for you.

Write your thoughts and feelings in a letter. You will never give this to them, so don't hold back. Write out everything that has led to your decision, and explain your reasons for departing the relationship.

There is something immensely therapeutic about writing, and when you write openly and honestly without fear of repercussions, you can really heal some wounds inside yourself.

If you feel safe doing so, share with the person what led up to the decision. But only if you truly feel safe. I believe people deserve to know what went wrong in a relationship, rather than be ghosted and left with no answers. Of course, your mental, emotional, and physical safety should be considered in deciding whether or not to take this step.

If there could be retaliation or a harmful response, it's okay to skip this step. If you do feel safe to proceed, you can either express your intentions in a letter or have an actual conversation.

Cut off all communication. This one is nuanced, because some relationships require co-work after they are finished. Like co-parents or coworkers, for example. Cut off communication to the highest possible extent. If you must remain in contact, keep communication strictly to the topic of the thing you share. Whether it be your child, your work, your business, etc., only talk about that when necessary and nothing else.

If this is a relationship that's hurting you and holding you back, there is no point in keeping one foot in and one foot out.

Please note: if it's a romantic relationship you're leaving because it's no longer fulfilling but is still supportive, you *do not* need to cut all ties with this person. There is such a thing as being friends with your ex, and it can be a beautiful friendship if the circumstances are right.

Do a cord-cutting meditation. This step is all about energetically severing ties with the person who no longer has a place in your energetic field. Aligned energy helps you manifest better and live with purpose. A person who drains this energy holds you back from reaching your full potential.

- To do this meditation, settle into a relaxed state in a comfortable position and clear your mind. When you're settled into your meditation, visualize the person you are leaving behind. Visualize them far away from you, no longer affecting your emotional and mental energy.

- Next, see the cord that connects that person to you. It can be a rope, a light, or even an electrical wire. Notice where on your body this cord is connected to you—your heart, your stomach, your throat, or somewhere else. The place of connection can be symbolic of the chakra this relationship is blocking.

- Imagine a tool that will help you sever the cord. It can be a huge pair of scissors, a sword, a chainsaw, a lightsaber—it doesn't matter. Now, cut that damn cord. Cut it with intention, cut it with passion; and as you're cutting, repeat, "Disintegrate, disconnect." Do it over and over again until you feel satisfied.

- Once the cord is satisfactorily severed, imagine it lying there on the ground, limp and lifeless. Finally, visualize the powerless cord disintegrating and the person disappearing, until all you're left with is empty space and maybe a wound where the cord was connected that you'll have to heal over time.

This is a potent visualization, because it allows you to take back the power over any situation by energetically separating from it. You can use this cord-cutting meditation for cutting ties with more than just people. You can also use it for limiting beliefs, bad habits, and situations you no longer want to be a part of.

The letter you wrote that you weren't going to give to the person, either burn it or give it to them. Didn't I say it's a letter you'll never give to them? Yes. I want you to write as if you'll never give it to them. I don't want you to hold back. In fact, write it with the intention of burning it.

There is a certain finality to destroying something with fire, and it feels like a release. Before you burn it, though, read it over. You may feel called to give it to the person it's intended for. Do what feels right with that letter.

One thing I don't recommend, however, is keeping it. That's like storing old, stagnant, hurtful energy, and that's not beneficial at all.

Give yourself grace. Once the steps above are done, give yourself time to mourn the relationship. There is nothing left to do but to move on. For me, getting over a friendship takes longer and is a more sustained hurt than getting over a romantic relationship. After a romantic breakup, the pain is deep for a while, and then it starts to feel better. A friendship breakup, on the other hand, at least in my experience, is less deep, but it persists over a much longer period of time.

Usually, when we enter into a romantic relationship, we understand there's a decent chance of it not working out. I'm not sure why, but we don't look at friendships in the same way. We assume our friends will always be there in some capacity.

Sure, people drift apart, but the tumultuous partings take us by surprise, and the healing from such a breakup is not linear. I do think it depends a lot on the way the falling out happened. If there was a lot of anger, you need to reconcile those feelings.

Sometimes, writing the letter is enough, and sometimes, you need to do more work. For me, journaling helped me to move on and resolve my anger. I do still find myself thinking about my former friends years later. They cross my mind now and then, and I always stop the thought in its tracks, wish them well, and move on to the next thought.

Fear of Letting Go of the Facade

Another common fear that might not be obvious is the fear of letting go of the facade of external success. This one, I totally came up with myself, so chances are you won't find this in any textbook, but it's something real I experienced in my own journey to purpose. It might come up for you, too, so I want to point it out.

When I was leaving my life behind to start my six-month RV trip, I was leaving behind everything I had worked for. I had all the things society told me should make me happy, and by all standards I was successful. The status symbols of success were all there—the house, the cars, the designer handbags, all of it. And I really had worked hard to achieve that. I had dreamed of this life, and I'd been envious of others when they got there before I did.

That's why, in my mind, it was so hard to reconcile leaving it all behind. It wasn't so much about what others would think of me. This fear was more internal. My outward-facing success was everything I'd strived for my entire life. But when I got there, to the peak of it, I felt empty and exhausted. It took so much to keep up with everything! Cleaning my house took hours, mowing the lawn and cleaning up the yard took up a whole day, the pool turned green when we went on vacation, and taxes, my God, the taxes! We lived in Connecticut, so we had a car tax and a property tax that ended up costing us multiple-five figures per year.

Some would say we couldn't afford the lifestyle we were living, and to that I say: I 100% agree. But as humans, socially conditioned to want nice things and appear successful, we did it anyway. The constant worry of what would happen if the shit hit the fan did not feel good, but I feared what it would mean for my success, if I didn't have the outward symbols to show it.

I knew we weren't meant to stay there, in that frequency of always chasing, chained to the work we didn't love, just to maintain it all. So, when we sold the Denali and I felt a wave of freedom come over me, I knew we had to get rid of all of it. It wasn't easy. Logistically, mentally, emotionally, physically, it was one of the hardest things I've ever done, leaving behind all the stuff I'd spent my whole life acquiring. But it was freeing.

And now, almost a year later, I don't even think about the stuff. I have about ninety-percent less than I used to, and I never feel like I lack anything. And it turns out that not having symbols of success to show off does not take away from the success at all! In fact, I would argue it has made me *more* successful.

When you get comfortable with your purpose and decide to take ownership of your happiness, you may be faced with a similar decision. Stuff holds us back. It demands a lot of our energy by requiring maintenance and financial commitment, and it takes up physical space. It puts us in a closed-off energetic frequency, because there's no room for new things to enter. When you begin to let go of the old stuff, you have the opportunity to bring in better, newer, more aligned stuff.

The Common Denominator of Fear

Predictability makes us feel warm and fuzzy inside. When we live the same day over and over again, it may be boring, but it is dependable and familiar, and that's comforting.

Predictability is addicting, because our brains are wired to seek it.

Back in our hunter-gatherer days, we had to worry about survival; those who lived the boring lives in the predictable environments, doing the same thing day in and day out, were the ones who survived. They lived to pass along their boringness-craving genes, and thus here we are, stuck living the same day over and over again to avoid being mauled by a saber tooth tiger.

Predictability allows us control over the unknown. Staying in your hometown after you grow up, sticking with your stable yet excruciatingly dull job, refusing to leave a relationship that fizzled out years ago—these all make your life exceptionally predictable and comfortable. Your brain doesn't have to work very hard to know what to expect next, which makes things easy.

The fear of letting go of control keeps people paralyzed in a life of emptiness. If you really boil down all the other fears I've discussed in this chapter, you will find the fear of letting go of control at the bottom of the pot.

Fear of failure = inability to control outcomes
Fear of what others will think = inability to control others' perceptions of you
Fear of not being enough = inability to control your own self-worth
Fear of what will change = inability to control the unknown
Fear of letting go of the facade = inability to control how you are validated

This is the root of all our fears: uncertainty. And it's powerful. Uncertainty keeps us stuck, paralyzed even, with fear that, if we move, we will fail in some way. What if I leave my hometown and can't make connections or find a job? What if I leave my boring job and the thing that I'm passionate about doesn't make me enough money? What if I leave my unfulfilling relationship and end up alone forever? What if, what if, what if...?

Well, what if it *does* all work out? We tend to "what if" the worst-case scenario to death, but we rarely consider with any conviction the best-case scenario. This is because we think more about what we fear than what we desire. It's called *negativity bias*, and it's yet another survival mechanism we inherited from our ancient ancestors. It kind of feels like the Neanderthals were trying to sabotage our success with all these bad habits they evolved for us, doesn't it?

Negativity bias means we pay more attention to and resonate more deeply with our negative experiences than our positive ones. Our ancestors always had negativity on their minds as they scanned their environment for threats.

"The snake that bit my neighbor, who died the next day, it had a red stripe across its body."

"The berry that made me throw up like crazy eight-and-a-half years ago, it grew on a shrub with heart-shaped leaves."

They remembered the minute details of the threats they'd encountered, and this helped them to survive. But this instinct also made them extra careful. "This berry looks just like the one that made me sick, but the leaves are not heart-shaped. Better stay away from it just in case."

Since we can be fairly confident that the grocery store is not trying to poison us, we don't have to pay as much attention to our food and our environment. Our survival is more or less guaranteed on a day-to-day basis now, so we apply this carefulness to other areas in our lives—like staying in unfulfilling jobs and relationships. We still like familiarity, because it feels safe.

Fear, despite the actual threat, feels a lot more intense and immediate than desire does. When we contemplate making a major life change and the "what ifs" creep in, we mentally play out those scenarios as if those things are happening in the here and now. Emotions kick in immediately, and we panic.

When we visualize desires, on the other hand, the emotions don't come automatically. We need to tap into the emotions associated with reaching our desires, but the whole concept feels like a distant dream rather than an immediate reality. In truth, however, both the fear and the desire are the same distance away from you. They're both plausible, and they're both equally likely to happen.

So, what do we do? How do we let go of fear, so it doesn't paralyze us? The answer is not super-satisfying. Unfortunately, I don't have a tried-and-true method for eliminating fear. That's because we cannot truly eliminate it. It's an instinct, and it does serve a purpose, so never experiencing fear would not be in our best interest.

It's simple. The only way to overcome fear is to understand it, acknowledge it, and move through it. It's the only way to reach your ideal self: the more you make moves despite the fear, the easier it will be to make moves despite the fear.

So, befriend your fear, and invite it to come along with you on your journey to your ideal reality. Do the thing that scares you the most, because the best rewards are on the other side of that fear.

CHAPTER 10

Designing Your Purpose Activation Blueprint

AT THIS POINT, you've done the work, you've learned about the mindset you need, you've considered your fears, and you know you need to quantum leap. Now, let's put together your Purpose Activation Blueprint.

If you wrote on loose pages or in a blank notebook, I'd like you to compile all of the pages you wrote for the activities in the prior chapters. Keep them arranged in the same order you worked on them. If you wrote in the *Purpose Activation Blueprint Workbook*, your instructions are laid out clearly in the "Designing Your Purpose Activation Blueprint" section.

Next, we will analyze your responses, looking for themes and sentiments.

The goal of this section is to provide you with a clear roadmap to fulfilling your purpose and living a satisfying life. I will guide you in extracting keywords and themes from your responses, and I will show you how to string them together to form a coherent plan for your life's purpose.

There are several things to consider, however. The information I am providing here is general, meaning it is intended to be interpretable by many different people from many walks of life. Your specific circumstances should be considered in your analysis and conclusions.

For example, if you determine your purpose is to create art, your next step is to consider how living this purpose could look in your own life. If you're someone who is well-off financially, this could mean creating art for your own personal development and/or maybe donating your work and time to raise money for philanthropic causes. If you're not in a situation where you could live without an income, you'll need to consider how your purpose fits into your life while still earning a salary. Perhaps teaching art to others could be an option, or art could be your purpose-filling hobby outside of your income-producing work.

Of course, there is no way I could identify each and every avenue one could take in fulfilling their life's purpose. This part of the process requires intimate understanding of someone's situation. For my clients, this work is done one-on-one. For the purposes of this book, however, I will leave this part of the analysis up to you.

The next section will outline the steps I recommend you take to analyze the reflective work you've completed in the previous sections. The intention here is to identify recurring themes in your responses, which will ultimately point you toward your life's purpose.

Here we go.

Creating your Blueprint

If you're using *The Purpose Activation Blueprint Workbook*, the instructions are all outlined there for you. You can skip this part and work directly in the workbook. When you're finished, you can go straight to the next section, "Purpose in Action."

If you are working in a blank notebook, you'll need several pages for this part.

Step 1:

Read all of your responses thoroughly, in order from the beginning, and highlight or underline words or phrases that you feel are important and/or revealing.

Step 2:

Look through the words and phrases you've highlighted and write them out on a separate sheet of paper. Identify any repetition by combining similar words and making a tick mark for each mention of a similar concept (for example: visible/invisible/feeling seen III). This step is meant to call your attention to the recurring sentiments you've gathered. The ones you see repeated over and over are telling. Keep those top of mind as you go through the next steps.

Step 3:

Set up the following categories each on a separate page: Core Motivations, Innate Strengths, Transformed Pain, Highest Impact, and Legacy.

Then, go back to your written responses from the previous chapters, and write the keywords and phrases you've identified in the prompts associated with each category based on the list below.

Finally, respond to the prompt listed under each category below.

Core Motivations (Why you're driven to act)
- Challenging Core Beliefs (Ch. 2)
- Values List (Ch. 3)
- The Five Whys (Ch. 3)
- The Should vs. Want Exercise (Ch. 3)

Identify the emotional drivers behind your recurring themes. Highlight motivations like impact, connection, growth, or freedom.

Innate Strengths (What comes naturally to you)
- Strength Journaling (Ch. 4)
- Skills and Strengths Inventory (Ch. 4)
- Flow State Reflection (Ch. 4)
- Journaling: The Peak Experiences (Ch. 5)

Which skills or talents feel easy, energizing, and effective? Prioritize those that overlap with flow states and peak experiences.

Transformed Pain (What you've overcome)
- Reflecting on Limiting Beliefs (Ch. 2)
- Childhood Reflection (Ch. 5)
- Triggers Journal (Ch. 6)
- Childhood Memory Exercise (Ch. 6)
- Revisiting Old Wounds (Ch. 6)

Identify patterns of struggle or formative pain that have shaped your empathy, insight, or desire to help others. These often point toward who you're here to serve.

Highest Impact (Who you're meant to help and how)
- Flow State Analysis (Ch. 5)
- Need Mapping Visualization (Ch. 7)
- Needs-to-Purpose Bridge Exercise (Ch. 7)
- Recognize Your Unique Contribution (Ch. 8)
- Explore Barriers to Service (Ch. 8)

Look for language tied to impact, transformation, or unmet needs. What problem are you naturally equipped to solve? Who benefits most from your presence?

Legacy (What future you're building)
- Ideal Self Visualization (Ch. 2)
- Mood Tracking (Ch. 5)
- Personality Alignment Inventory (Ch. 7)
- Visualize Your Ideal Legacy (Ch. 8)

Identify themes related to long-term vision. Highlight where your future self, values, and ideal impact converge. Look for emotional resonance. What future feels expansive?

Step 4:

Review your responses for Reflecting on Limiting Beliefs (Ch. 2) and Challenging Core Beliefs (also Ch. 2). These exercises help you see that many of your limiting beliefs are not based on facts. They are assumptions you've been conditioned to believe or reflections of past experiences.

- Identify beliefs that may be holding you back, and reflect on where these beliefs come from. Some common examples of limiting beliefs are fear of failure, self-worth issues, fear of being seen, or societal pressures to perform/look/behave a certain way.

- Brainstorm ways to overcome your limitations. Since these are all internal beliefs, the work necessary to overcome them must come from within you. You might consider getting into a routine of journaling, EFT tapping, visualization, and/or meditation.

Step 5:

From the Explore Barriers to Service (Ch. 8) exercise, determine what internal or external barriers are preventing you from fully realizing your purpose.

- Think about where the barriers originated, which ones are real and which ones are perceived, and what the version of you looks like who is already living on the other side of overcoming these barriers.

- Brainstorm how you can overcome your barriers. If they are real, think about how to get around them practically (learning new skills, enrolling in a course, networking with influential people, etc.). And if they're perceived, you can use journaling, EFT tapping, visualization, and/or meditation here, too.

Step 6:

Through the Visualize Your Ideal Legacy (Ch. 8) exercise and Recognizing Your Unique Contribution (also Ch. 8), think about how you see yourself serving others and the impact you want to leave behind.

- Think about what you are here to express or create, who you are here to impact, what would change in the lives of others if you were to live your purpose fully without holding back, and what kind of emotional or energetic imprint you want to leave on others.
- Brainstorm ways to leave your imprint on the world. When your time on Earth is finished, will you leave behind something tangible, like art or a book? Or will you leave behind people who have been touched by your work? Maybe a combination of both?

Step 7:

Create your Purpose Statement. With a clearer understanding of your strengths, values, passions, and limiting beliefs, you can now craft a purpose statement that encapsulates your insights.

Using the information gathered, write a concise statement that reflects your purpose. This could be one sentence or a short paragraph that encompasses all areas of the Purpose Activation Blueprint. Start with the following framework and expand as needed:

"My purpose is to [what you want to do], using my strengths in [list your strengths] to make a positive impact on [who or what you want to help]."

Purpose in Action

Congratulations! You've completed the process for identifying your life's purpose. Now, the next phase of the project begins: taking action. This is the part of the process that will be the most unique to you and your needs.

I'm going to give you a basic framework of what you should consider and how to start moving your feet toward your purpose, but it will be your job to figure out how to do it in a way that fits your lifestyle and needs.

It's also important to note that you cannot possibly plan every single detail. The whole point of aligning with your higher self is to open yourself up to opportunities that the future you recognizes and takes. I strongly advise you *not* to plan too hard, because that puts you in a clingy state of lack, which actually repels opportunities from you. The sweet spot is to approach this with intention and flexibility. Have a vision of the outcome, but don't worry too much about the details, and take aligned action whenever an opportunity presents itself. With that being said, let's take a look at some of the steps you'll need to take to get moving toward your purpose.

First, outline what you'll need to do. I don't like the word *goals* because for a goal to be effective, there needs to be a timeline attached. In my work, I've learned that detaching from timelines is actually what makes our desires flow in faster. For our purposes here, I'm going to use the word *intentions*. Break down your purpose statement into both long-term and short-term intentions. This should be a list of outcomes, not a to-do list.

For example, if you intend to quit your job (sorry, I can't stop telling people to quit their jobs!), I want you to write "quit my job" as the intention, not "find and train a suitable replacement so my boss will be okay when I leave" or "finish XYZ project, wait until the New Year, then hand in my resignation letter." Don't let yourself get bogged down by the details, or the "how."

Next, brainstorm some activities or projects you can do that align with your purpose. This can include things like volunteering in the space that aligns with your passion, starting a blog or social media channel to find your voice, pursuing a side hustle that reflects your purpose, or taking classes to help you develop relevant skills. The intention here is to put yourself physically into a space that aligns with your purpose. You might be surprised by the opportunities that begin to show up just because you were in the right place at the right time with the right people. This is the most important part of the action process.

Finally, reflect and adjust regularly. We'll go into more detail on this one later. Your purpose can evolve over time, and it's essential to regularly revisit and adjust your Purpose Activation Blueprint. Schedule regular check-ins on your calendar to reflect on your progress toward your goals. I happen to be intuitive to moon cycles, so with every new moon, I take some time to reflect on the last moon cycle and what I've accomplished. Then, I set intentions for the new cycle. This happens roughly every thirty days, and I take the whole day to reflect, meditate, and journal.

Checking in with yourself is important because, sometimes, we can get really caught up in the "doing" part, and we might actually be moving in the wrong direction.

These regular check-ins help to catch those misguided moves and get you back on track.

I know this well because I purchased a (very expensive) course once where I was taught that focusing on promoting a high-touch, one-on-one program is the best way to start a coaching business. The sales strategy involved a ton of cold messaging and follow-up to get people interested in the program.

Before I started this course, I had set out to release Mindful Manifest Flow, my ten-week meditation series for aligning with your higher self that I described earlier. This was the program that helped me free myself of the life that no longer served me, and I wanted to share it with the world. But I put that on the back burner and tried to promote a high-ticket coaching program that I didn't even have anything prepared for, because the coach who had produced this course was successful in starting up her business this way. I basically did what I was instructed to do because I believed in replicating successful processes to become successful. It's worked for me before in other lines of work!

The problem with that mindset, however, when it comes to aligning with your purpose, is you can't replicate someone else's method. Your purpose and your way of living it are unique, and no one else can do it the way you do. Purpose-driven work isn't like other businesses, where there is a proven system and all you have to do is follow the steps. Your process needs to be right for you, and even though someone else had success doing things a certain way, it does not mean that strategy will work for you.

When I was operating from this inauthentic version of myself, I was feeling very off. My temper was short, I was stressed out, I wasn't feeling creative, and, worst of all, I was not feeling motivated to work on my business. I almost gave up. The cold messaging was the worst part of my day. I was not good at it, and when people actually responded to my opening message (which was not often), I found myself not knowing what to say. I'm not a salesy person, and this felt very misaligned for me.

In my monthly reflection, I realized I had abandoned the very thing that drove my purpose and set me on this path: Mindful Manifest Flow. I knew this program was extremely powerful, and I already had evidence of its potency because I saw how quickly my own life turned around when I did the meditation series myself. I knew instantly that I needed to shift gears and put my focus back on my signature program. The coaching would come later and more naturally. So, I deleted the cold-messaging task from my recurring to-do list, I reorganized my sales page and added a waitlist for Mindful Manifest Flow, and I put all of my energy toward getting the program together and releasing it into the world.

My energy shifted immediately. John noticed right away. The very next day after my revelation, he asked, "What changed? You're back to your old self!" I love the fact that he didn't ask what was wrong with me when I was misaligned. He trusts that, when I can verbalize my problems, I will tell him. I operate in my own head for the most part, so oftentimes, when I'm feeling off, I don't know why right away. But when I figure it out, I share it with him, and he gives me the space to do so.

The point of my story is to show you how I was working toward my purpose—helping people to align with their higher selves—but not in the right way. I did eventually start coaching, but I'm so glad I waited for the right time. And I'm not done with developing my program yet, but the shifts away from Mindful Manifest Flow happened because of alignment (like writing this book and moving to Spain, for example) and not forcing something inauthentic. There is still *so much* more to come!

I'm so glad I checked in with myself and quickly found that I was misaligned. I came really close to giving up, feeling like I didn't have it in me to do what was necessary for success! If you find yourself in a similar frame of mind, please, please, please think back to this page and remember that there is more than one way to do just about everything. If what you're trying isn't working, *Do Not Give Up!* Adjust something, and try again. The only way to fail is to give up.

Surrendering to Your Purpose

I've learned in my experience with manifestation and purpose-seeking that the more you try to control the outcomes, the further your desires float away from your reality. Control stems from a mindset based in scarcity and fear, because you are essentially embodying the idea that there is not enough to go around. When you try to plan every detail of the desire you want to call into your life, you are essentially reinforcing the belief that resources and opportunities are limited, and in order to get your piece of the pie, you must accomplish X, Y, and Z.

You're micromanaging the higher power when you try to guess how your desires will show up or the sequence of events that will lead up to an opportunity or an accomplishment. You're showing that you don't trust the process. You're also limiting yourself, because, more often than not, the Universe has bigger plans for you than you can even dream of, and when you're attached to a certain outcome, you may be cutting off energy to the flow of something bigger and better.

It's an easy trap to fall into, because most of the manifestation techniques involve some form of imagery of your desired outcome. The natural progress of the visualization is to pinpoint how the desire may come about. If you imagine yourself with a million dollars, you will get naturally curious about how you acquired the money, and you'll start to imagine the various paths to that outcome.

I cannot stress this enough: you are limiting yourself when you start dissecting the desire. Your only job in manifestation is to be clear on the desire (not how you obtain it) and then to align with the version of you who has achieved it.

The best way to manifest is to lead with feeling. Imagine how your life *feels* when you've manifested your desires, not just how it looks. Tune into the vibrational frequency of the ease money brings, the joy of a family, or the sense of accomplishment following a major win. Ignore the *how*. Just pay attention to the emotional state you want to live in.

Also, it seems kind of counterintuitive, but you have to be emotionally and energetically okay with your desire *not* showing up in your life. You can still want it, but you cannot be desperate for it. In other words, you have to remain neutral. Desperation is lack, and it will repel your desire.

This process is called *surrender*, and it requires full trust that the Universe is working behind the scenes to give you what you want, even if you can't see it in your external reality yet. When you surrender, you are actively releasing control of how and when things will unfold. This results in true alignment with abundance.

This process works for manifesting anything you want—money, love, success, anything—but it's easier said than done, and it can only be used for the highest good, not harm. Manifesting requires absolute trust that your desire is on its way to you without any inkling of proof in your external reality. In fact, there might be proof to the contrary in your life, but in order to successfully manifest, you must act as if, without a shadow of a doubt, the desire will appear in perfect timing.

The word *surrender* tends to have a negative connotation—like giving up or doing nothing—but this is not the intention here at all. The trick behind surrender is to let go of the desperation and attachment, but pay attention to your surroundings and respond to opportunities. Just like in pursuing your purpose, manifestation requires aligned action.

After you set your intention, pay attention to who enters into your life and what opportunities appear. There are always signs pointing you in the right direction; you just need to be aware enough to identify them.

When taking aligned action, this is where the real test comes in. To truly move toward your desire, you must have no attachment to and no expectations of the outcome resulting from the action you're taking. You have to just do it because it feels aligned, and trust that it is for your highest good. If it wasn't, you would not be called to it.

The hardest part is moving with no confirmation that your actions are bringing you closer to your desires. This is trust. This is faith. And if you can master this, the rewards are insane.

The good news, though, is that there often are signs indicating you're on the right track. You might see repeating numbers or other personally meaningful signs in your environment to give you encouragement, but the most important sign to look out for is how you feel. If you feel calm and at ease, you're probably headed in the right direction. If you're feeling stressed or frustrated, you probably need to change something.

Nervousness is okay if it's something new and exciting, but there's a difference between feeling nervous and feeling anxious. I do trust you will know the difference in your own body, but if you have trouble, I suggest you do my favorite thing ever: journal on it.

Mastering the art of surrender is an absolute game changer for manifestation. It brings you into alignment without much effort, and your desires will start showing up like rapid fire. I've learned to put my own spin on surrender and make it easy by using mindfulness.

In essence, this is what Mindful Manifest Flow is about: using mindfulness as a form of surrender in manifestation. If this idea piques your interest, or you're new to manifestation and you'd like to learn more, I invite you to check out my website: themindfulwaypoint.com.

CHAPTER 11

Sustaining Purpose Over Time

JUST LIKE EVERYTHING else in life, purpose comes in seasons. It is not static and will change over time. This is another reason why regular check-ins are important. What feels aligned and purposeful right now might not feel that way in a few years or even a few months, as you grow and develop.

The ebbs and flows of purpose often follow a similar pattern based on your season of life. For example, in early adulthood, the primary focus is on identity and developing a sense of self. In adulthood, we focus on career and family and providing for our children. Those without children find other ways to leave a legacy and make an impact on their community. In midlife, we tend to reevaluate what we're doing, and, now financially stable, we move toward things that feel more personally fulfilling rather than what makes us money. Later in life, we shift toward doing something that will leave a lasting impact and/or a legacy for our children.

Evolving Purpose

The evolutionary cycle of purpose follows Erik Erikson's theory of psychosocial development, which highlights the importance of personal development coupled with social influences. This is important to consider, because it can help you understand why certain things that used to feel fulfilling no longer do so. Your level of service to others will also ebb and flow, moving from minimal desire to serve others in early adulthood to focusing on your own family or other impactful contribution in adulthood and, finally, to a wider reach of serving in later adulthood, when impactful work for the greater good becomes a major focus.

It's also important to note that major life changes can impact purpose. Health issues, death of a loved one, or a major move can greatly affect how you align with your purpose. In these moments, you may redefine purpose to align with the new circumstances. It's important to assess how you're feeling following a major life shift and adjust, if things begin to feel misaligned.

And finally, purpose can be multifaceted in different stages of life. There can be synchronicity in doing fulfilling work and raising children, or raising children can be the purpose while work takes a back seat for some time. The work that feels fulfilling can also shift over time.

While there usually are some underlying factors, there are times when purpose truly changes. For example, you might be compelled to create art in early adulthood and that feels purposeful and fulfilling. As you shift to later adulthood and need to provide for your growing family, you might begin working in a different career that brings in more money, and you might find passion in your new line of work, while your art falls to the wayside. That new work could be your purpose for the rest of your working years, and then you'll return to your art in retirement. This is totally acceptable, too.

The point here is that purpose does not follow any certain trajectory. While there are some foundational rules, there is a lot of variety in how purpose shows up and how it is sustained for different people. To demonstrate this, I'd like to share with you the evolution of my purpose. I've discussed some details of my journey already, but here I will put them in order and identify the things leading up to the decisions that got me to where I am. My intention is to provide you with a real example of how purpose evolves. I hope you can find some connection to my story.

As I've mentioned, my purpose is teaching others. Thinking back on the evolution of my purpose, I can pinpoint several times in my life when I found fulfillment in teaching and training, without even knowing this was my purpose. My first job was at an ice cream shop when I was sixteen years old. I really enjoyed that job, and I was a hard worker. Eventually, I was asked to train new employees, and this was where I found the job most fulfilling.

In college, I started bartending. As a young adult, I was most fulfilled by the insane money I was making and the fun I was having. Interestingly, when I was asked to train a new person in this line of work, I often found it burdensome. For anyone who has ever worked in a busy restaurant or bar, you know what I'm talking about. It sucks to be the new person, trying to keep up, and it sucks even more to be responsible for that new person, because your own work becomes much harder. In my selfish young-adult phase, I did *not* like teaching others.

After college, I started working at an insurance company. I've already shared this story with you. A quick recap: the work was awful, but when I started training new hires, I felt fulfilled. Although I knew I couldn't stay there long because it was soul-sucking work for me, I considered transitioning to the training department. When I learned that was not an option, I bounced right over to grad school.

In my mid-twenties, while I was in school, I went back to restaurant work for the money. This time, though, the money was less important than school. In college, I could work until 4:00 a.m. and go to class at 8:00, hungover, and it would be fine. "A 'C' is a degree," I would say to myself. The bare minimum was sufficient.

I could *not* do that in grad school. I had to stick with the 10:00 p.m. closing-time shifts. I got married while in grad school and started to think about buying a house and having kids. My focus shifted from lots of money and fun to just making ends meet while getting my career started.

My graduate work was in school psychology. My plan was to work in the school systems until I retired with a government pension. The driving factor during this part of my life was stability and financial security. No one gets rich working in a public school, but there are great benefits, and you get summers off. I thought this was perfect for when I had kids.

Lo and behold, I hated the actual job. My Generator intuition tells me immediately when something is not right for me. I knew it in my insurance job before I even finished training for the job, and I knew it in grad school before I finished my practicum.

I think supporting students is necessary work, and I was excited to make a difference in kids' lives while learning the theory behind it. I had not had much experience with kids at this point, and I wasn't positive I would like working with them, but I thought that making a difference and impacting futures would be the fulfilling part.

Boy, was I wrong. The job itself was more difficult than I'd expected. I give a lot of credit to teachers and anyone working in the public schools. It's not for the faint of heart! The days are long, the work is repetitive, and it doesn't end when the final bell rings. There are reports to write at home, meetings to attend, school politics to deal with, etc. I could see how the work would be fulfilling, and I definitely had some feel-good moments when I was able to make a small difference in a child's life, but it turned out I didn't really like working with kids, and I liked dealing with the parents even less. Call me a quitter, but I had to bow out.

Next up, it was time to quit my grad program. I had just finished my master's degree and had one year to go for the sixth-year certificate to complete the program, but there was no sense in continuing. I knew it wasn't for me. When I had this difficult conversation with my program advisors, I was terrified. Imagine telling someone who has dedicated their entire life to this field, has published textbooks on the subject, and believes this is the most impactful work there is that you couldn't hack it and you're out. I thought they were going to chew me up. To my surprise, however, after some attempts at convincing me to stick it out, I was offered a job.

It was an adjunct role teaching Intro to Psychology to freshmen (or first-years, as they are now called). The pay was shit, but it was only a couple days a week, and *Professor* Oquendo had a nice ring to it. I signed up, and the very next year, I was offered a more permanent position in the department that combined teaching with some administrative tasks and advising students.

I realized I loved teaching! I was close in age to my students, and they really liked our conversations. I was a tough grader, though, which they did not usually appreciate. In this role, I learned that no matter how much some people love you, there will always be those who hate you. You cannot possibly appeal to every single person, and the bigger your reach, the more hate you will get. I've carried that with me ever since. It helps to know that this is inevitable and happens to everyone.

My job was so sweet. I got to work three days a week and had four months off in the summer, plus five weeks in the winter between semesters. To make it a full-time income, I picked up extra classes that I taught online during the summer and winter terms. Although the money wasn't great, it was not extraordinarily hard work, and I actually really enjoyed it. So much so that I decided to try to get into a PhD program, so I could teach full time and be important. (No one cares about what someone with a master's degree has to say in academia.) I applied to *one* program, got denied, and then Covid hit.

Covid flipped the world on its head, and my job was no exception. We had to go remote for half of the fall semester in 2020 and during all of the spring. I actually loved that part, because I am a huge fan of working from home, but I knew it was not a great teaching model. I could see the decline in quality of work my students were submitting. When we returned to campus in fall 2021, it was just different. I had spent almost a whole year not being face-to-face with students, and I thought I had lost my charm, as a result. I kept trying to connect with my students the way I had pre-Covid, but it just wasn't working.

The students didn't show up for class like they used to (an email claiming they were "not feeling well" was enough to get an excused absence, per university policy), and there were days when I'd be talking to a room of two or three students for an hour and a half. When they did show up, the conversations were not as engaging as they used to be.

I think one reason for the disconnection was the fact that our age gap was increasing. When I started teaching, I was an elder millennial teaching younger millennials. When Gen Z entered the room, I was officially old and out of touch.

Another factor was probably their high school experience, which had been interrupted by Covid. I remember how important socializing was in high school, and I can only imagine what a whole year away from friends does to the social development of a teenager. I bet there are studies on this by now. Either way, the disconnect I was feeling was a blow to my ego, and I quickly started to lose interest in teaching.

In the background of all this, I was working in real estate, first as a realtor and later as an investor. This part of my story has its own arc, but for the sake of staying on topic, I'll be brief. I never considered real estate to be my purpose-driven work. I thought it could be when I started, but soon realized it was only meant to be an investment strategy. It did, in fact, align nicely with my need to take care of my family. As an investment, real estate helped set us up for long-term wealth, and that continues to be a major focus of mine as I build out strategies to secure my children's futures.

I hope you're seeing the pattern of how passion and purpose can change over time. Even jobs we love and purposeful work can begin to feel burdensome after some time. In my case, so far, it has been in part due to situations outside my control (aging, Covid, etc.), but also in part due to the Universe telling me to keep it moving. When I found things that I really enjoyed doing within the things I didn't enjoy so much, I made attempts at staying put in a more aligned way, but ultimately, I failed. When those doors did not open when I tried them, I didn't keep knocking. I moved on quickly.

My experience of working from home during Covid was so nice, I decided my next move was going to be in that direction. I can see why my generation was so reluctant to return to the office after Covid. I loved being home with my daughter, working in my PJs, eating lunch prepared from my fridge, and sneaking off early or in the middle of the day to do stuff with my family. (This is why I make a terrible employee. I do my work and I do it well, but I like to make my own rules.) My purpose had shifted at this point toward being home and present for my daughter. Finding work that allowed me this luxury became of utmost importance, and teaching fell to the wayside.

Enter: bookkeeping. I was researching work-from-home gigs, and I learned about remote bookkeeping. I didn't know much about accounting other than the absolute basics from the records I'd kept on my rental properties for my tax returns. There were courses that claimed they could teach you the profession from start to finish, and you'd be making $100,000 a year. It sounded great, but we weren't quite in a financial position to invest in that. I let that idea simmer while I continued working at the university and supplementing my income by working in a restaurant one or two nights a week.

One day, I got to talking with a coworker at the restaurant, and she mentioned that she did bookkeeping as a side gig. I told her it was an interest of mine, but I didn't know the first thing about it. She said she would love to do it full time, but she wasn't sure about the business side of things. Entrepreneur lacking experience, meet Experience lacking entrepreneurial skills. I convinced her to go all in with me.

We became successful pretty quickly. The work was consistent, and we were growing based on word of mouth. We never even had to do any advertising. My son was born as the business was growing. I took unpaid maternity leave from my job at the university, and I was happy to have the flexibility of running my bookkeeping business from home on my own schedule and to be with my kids when I needed to be. This definitely aligned with what I needed in that moment.

A few years later, when my kids were a bit more independent, I expanded into tax work. I trucked along, doing accounting and working at the university, where my foot was increasingly out the door. Did I need both jobs? Not really. But the more money I made, the more stuff we upgraded, so I became stuck.

I became stuck in a cycle of consumerism, where there was never enough money to pay all the loans that I'd taken out on all the stuff I had acquired. I *had* to work both jobs, whether I wanted to or not.

In the background of all this, I was working on my psychotherapy license, and I was informally life-coaching people periodically before I became licensed. In the midst of chasing my tail, this was the only work that was actually fueling my passion.

After my dad died, I realized I was in a very stagnant place, surrounded by a lot of stuff. I saw how I was living beyond my means and not fulfilled by the status symbols I had acquired. My $100,000 SUV sat in the driveway with nowhere to go, because I was always working. My brand-new hot tub was mostly unused because, by the end of the day, I was so tired that asking me to change into my bathing suit was like asking me to climb Mt. Everest. My house rarely hosted guests because almost everyone had left my life at this point. I was killing myself, working so much for nothing. All while my kids were being schlepped back and forth to my mom's house for babysitting. I missed my time with them, and I definitely did not feel aligned.

I knew I had to change something. When I learned about and started practicing mindfulness meditation as a way to cope with the stress of being my father's caretaker at the end of his life, I began to intentionally change my mindset. I started weeding out the things that were not fulfilling and did not spark passion. This started with my job at the university and ended with almost every single thing I owned, when I sold it all to live on the road for six months.

I finally began to align with my purpose again, time with my family being at the forefront. From this mindset shift came the desire to teach others to also find their purpose, and I decided to start coaching. From there I decided to write this very book, and right now, as I write this sentence, I am living my purpose.

You can see from my career development that I was driven by many factors. There was my natural aging and maturing, which followed Erikson's psychosocial stages theory; there were major life changes, and there was a shift in what serving others meant to me.

Will this always be my purpose? I have no idea. I do feel I am in a genuine place and I am being my authentic self, living up to my values, using my strengths and experiences, working with passion, and serving others. I think this might be the first time all the boxes are checked, so I can see some version of this work being my purpose for the rest of my life.

I recommend revisiting your past work in a timeline, kind of like I did for myself here. The following prompt will help guide you in this reflection.

Reflection Prompt: Revisiting Your Career Path Through the Lens of Purpose

Take a moment to reflect on your past career journey. Think back to each major role, project, or position you've held. As you do, consider the following questions:

Identify Patterns and Themes: What common themes can you identify as you look back on your career trajectory? Are there specific types of tasks, roles, or industries that appear consistently? Some examples could include leadership roles, teaching, creative projects, or roles focused on supporting others. List these recurring patterns.

Emotional States Associated with Each Role: For each important role or project you took on, identify the primary emotions you experienced. Did you feel energized, fulfilled, and challenged? Or perhaps drained, frustrated, or overwhelmed? Consider what it was about each role that sparked these emotions and what they reveal about your personal needs.

Alignment with Your Purpose Activation Blueprint: Reflecting on your Blueprint, evaluate each role:
- Did it align with your core values?
- Did it allow you to use your strengths and pursue your passions?
- Did you feel you were making a meaningful impact?

How to Know You're on the Right Track

When you start the work of living your true, authentic purpose, there will be signs that you're on the right track. Your general sense of happiness and fulfillment and excitement will be your first sign. You will feel energized by the tasks and projects that are bringing you closer to your purpose. A task that might have felt like a chore when it was done for other goals will no longer feel tedious. It's a weird transition, but let me give you an example.

When I was working as a realtor, I did a lot of networking and marketing for myself. I talked to strangers and tried to get them to trust me with their real estate transaction. I hated it. It felt forced, I didn't feel confident or competent, and I wasn't good at it. For the most part, people didn't hire me, and those who did take a chance were sorely let down.

I remember a listing I took for a little ranch house owned by the parents of my coworker. It was the summer of 2017, and I spent countless beautiful Sundays hosting open houses and trying to market this house. It was not moving. After the summer ended and our contract expired, the owner said he'd like to take it off the market and do some improvements. A couple weeks later, I saw the house listed with another agent. To my surprise, the house sold soon after. There were no improvements made, the price was similar to mine, and the listing looked almost identical. What I had struggled (and failed) to do in six months, this new guy did in six weeks.

The work I did as a realtor was not aligned for me from the very beginning. I was drawn to it because I enjoyed real estate, but what I didn't realize at the time is that I enjoyed investing in real estate, not marketing and selling it. When I did eventually find my groove on the investment side, I was still networking and talking to people, but the conversations felt different. As an investor, I could be more laid back and less professional. Realtors need everyone to like them, so they need to be charismatic and eager to please in order to earn money, which is their objective. Investors don't care who likes them, because they're the ones with the purse. I liked it better this way, and my success grew quickly because I was doing work aligned with my personality.

You might notice a shift like this in your own work. At first, you might avoid doing something because it reminds you of a task you hate doing. I promise you, though, when the task is toward something aligned, it will not be difficult. It will actually feel enjoyable! I feel that way now about closing a sale in my coaching business. While I used to flounder when it came time to ask for money for my real estate services, I now confidently charge what I'm worth, and I have no issue asking for money because I know the value that I deliver to my clients.

There are common requirements for running a business. Marketing, closing a sale, managing finances, and maintaining connection with a client base are things every business needs to do to some extent. Similarly, every job has tasks that are less desirable, but when those tasks are being done in alignment with your purpose, they become more exciting and less tedious. It's a wonderful shift. When you begin to feel passion for things that once made you want to run for the hills, it means you're on the right track.

Another sign to look out for is losing track of time. This is the flow state I touched on earlier, and it's a great indicator that you're doing aligned work when you get so lost in it that time just feels... different. Time either goes by super-fast or super-slow. You either remember every detail of what you accomplished during that time, or it feels like a blur, like you were overtaken by something that did the work on your behalf. Either of these is great!

And finally, the most satisfying sign that you're aligned in your purpose: you become magnetic to the right people and opportunities. Seemingly out of nowhere, opportunities will start showing up that will help bring you closer to your purpose. People will show up in your life to teach you and mentor you in the right things. It's almost as if by magic that your circumstances begin to move you in the right direction.

Remember, though, a closed door does not open itself. You must remain receptive to the changes and allow the new people and opportunities to enter your life. Don't say, "It's not the right time," or "I'm not ready." If it's showing up, it means it *is* the right time, and you *are* ready.

Staying Aligned

Staying aligned with your purpose requires intentionality, self-reflection, and periodic realignment. When you're not being intentional, you are just existing. And you know what happens when you're just existing? You fall into a rut, your energy becomes depleted, and your relationships suffer.

When you are not fulfilled, you are not living up to your full potential. Being intentional requires checking in with yourself to make sure you are continuing to live in alignment with your higher self and making adjustments, if you're not.

Scheduling dedicated time to do this work is a must. If you're not consistent and you don't plan for it, you will always say, "I'll get to it soon." And then, you'll never get to it. The best way to get around this is to schedule time with yourself on your calendar. Once a month, for as much time as you need, sit down with your thoughts, and determine if you're still aligned and fulfilled.

Feelings of misalignment can hide beneath the perceived success of what you're doing, so it's easy to miss them, if you're doing well outwardly. Most people dismiss their feelings of misalignment, calling it burnout or "just a rough patch." Uhm, this might be shocking, but we're not supposed to feel burnt out by purposeful work. Burnout means there's something wrong and it needs to change immediately.

I recommend monthly check-ins to ensure you're still aligned with your higher self, not just in work but also in life in general. Some questions you can ask yourself are:

"Am I engaging in activities that align with my purpose?"

"Do my current roles and responsibilities feel meaningful?"

"Am I growing toward the goals that align with my core values and passions?"

"Am I currently doing and thinking the things my higher self does and thinks?"

That last question is important, because your environment responds to who you are being, per the Law of Attraction. If you want to have lots of money, you can't think and behave like a broke person. That energy repels money. You must embody the person you're trying to become.

You can do this by taking aligned and meaningful action on a regular basis. Even if you're not yet in a position where you could transition into your purpose, you can still take planned and consistent action toward it. This is achieved by setting daily and weekly intentions.

Ask yourself, "What can I do today/this week to live in alignment with my purpose?" This can be as simple as prioritizing one meaningful task each day that resonates with your larger vision. Over time, these tasks will stack up, and you'll be much closer to living your purpose. This is called *aligned action*.

You must also pay attention to what's happening in your environment. Life happens, and oftentimes major changes are the catalyst for major moves. When you experience significant life transitions, such as a job change, a new relationship, or a move, take time to reflect on whether your purpose needs adjustment. Use these moments as opportunities to reassess what feels meaningful and ensure your actions and choices still align with your purpose.

I like to keep track of all this reflection in my Purpose Journal. I keep two journals—one for manifestation, and one for purpose. In my Manifestation Journal, I write from the perspective of my future self, having achieved the goals I have now. I write from a place of accomplishment and gratitude. This helps me to align emotionally with success, thus attracting success to my current reality.

My other journal is where I do my reflective work, my intention-setting, and my gratitude practice. I write in my Purpose Journal both weekly and monthly. As I mentioned before, my monthly entries follow the moon cycles and consist of reflections on the last cycle and intentions for the new cycle. My weekly entries include gratitude for what I've accomplished and what I have in my life, as well as brainstorming things I could do in the upcoming week to bring me closer to my goals. Once I have a clear picture of what needs to be done, I write them out in "I will…" statements. This conviction helps to put some intentional energy behind the tasks.

I also journal on annual goals in my Purpose Journal. John and I have this tradition where we reflect on the past year on New Year's Eve and write out a goal list for the New Year. We also keep memory boxes for each year, where we add little souvenirs from things we experienced. They can be ticket stubs or maps of places we've visited, receipts from meaningful things we've purchased, and pictures our kids have drawn. On New Year's Eve, we look back at the goals we set a year ago and in years past, and we go through the memory box. We reminisce, and then we give the year a name, like, "The Year of [insert overarching theme here]." We will often go through the old memory boxes of years past, as well, to really put in perspective how far we've come.

The goals we set for the New Year range from likely-to-achieve to delusional. We've had "buy a Maserati" on the list for years now, but I have to say, we are closer to that goal than ever before. We *could* buy a Maserati right now, but other things are taking priority. I guess we'll have to reassess what's delusional for us in the upcoming New Year. It's fun to see the evolution of your priorities and the things you achieve over the years.

Another thing you'll have to do to align with your purpose is to leave behind the things and people holding you back. As I have mentioned, the shedding-people part was the hardest for me on my own journey. But it was necessary, and once I did it, the progress I made was insane. It really opened my eyes to how draining other people's energy can be.

It's important to assess periodically whether your relationships, commitments, and environment support your purpose. You have to surround yourself with people who encourage your growth, challenge you positively, and understand your values in an environment that is conducive to bringing you closer to your dreams.

Sometimes this means you will need a cleansing phase before *your people* enter your life. I can tell you from experience, cutting out negative people is both the hardest and most influential thing you can do toward your goals.

It does come as a shock, and I want you to be prepared for what is necessary, but the truth of the matter is this: you can't take everyone and everything with you into your future. You are a sum of your environment, and if you want change, you have to alter that equation.

The journey to true and sustainable change is a tough one. And I highly recommend you ask for help. Your friends will have a hard time supporting you through this molting process, because they will not understand it. If your journey ends up resembling mine, you might find yourself isolated and lonely. This is where a community of like-minded individuals can make all the difference for your well-being.

You can find a community like this on Facebook, from what I've seen, and the potent ones are accessible only through the purchase of a coaching program or course. You might find some free ones, and this might be a good place to start, but I've found that the paid ones are much more beneficial, because there are fewer trolls, and the leader of the group tends to be more active. I hope to create a group like this one day, because I wish I'd had one to connect with when I was feeling alone on my journey.

Another way to work through the isolation and uncertainty that comes with major life transformation is to hire help. There are lots of qualified and talented coaches who specialize in various areas. The trick is to find someone who is compatible. I've bought dozens of courses and hired a handful of coaches in my own journey, and I can tell you with certainty not all of them will be a good fit, and a higher price tag does *not* always equate to better quality.

I've found it's best to start by following a potential coach on social media, to get a sense of their personality, style, focus, and expertise. Most coaches offer a free or low-ticket course where you could get to know them a little better. The decision of who to hire requires about eighty percent intuition and twenty percent research. Some things to consider are:

> **Whether they offer practical advice and strategy or just motivation.** Some coaches are great at motivating you to make moves, but they leave the practical piece up to you entirely. This puts you totally in the driver's seat, and they act more like a source of inspiration and encouragement.

Others will help you come up with the game plan and will give you practical advice on how to implement it. They'll also check on your progress regularly and revisit the plan, to make sure it's working. (This is my coaching style, by the way.) Neither is right or wrong. It just depends on what you're looking for.

Understanding exactly what it is they're offering. For every problem, there are a million different solutions. And there are a million different coaches who teach each solution.

For example, if you're looking for career guidance, you might be choosing between a coach who will help you with your résumé, another who will help you with networking strategy, and another who will teach you meditation practices to tap into your intuition and follow your heart's desires. There are coaches who offer concrete strategy and advice and those who are more abstract in their practices. Again, both are fine. It's just a matter of what works best for you.

Making sure their values align with yours. This one can be difficult to spot through the fluff of advertising. Oftentimes, online coaches market themselves toward a specific pain point, and the social media algorithm puts them in front of people who experience that pain.

I don't know who needs to hear this, but social media knows you better than you know yourself, and they market products and services catered to your interests based on your scrolling history.

The problem with finding a coach is that coaching is expensive, and many coaches are not fully transparent about who they are and what they believe in their advertising. Their approach is to highlight your pain point in their ads and media content, so you're triggered and believe they can solve the problem for you. Then, when you buy into their services, you might realize it's not at all what you thought it would be and it's just not the right fit.

My best advice would be to follow the people you're potentially interested in working for a while. Watch their content and, even more important, watch their Instagram stories. Reels and posts are curated and well thought out, but stories are more spontaneous and intimate, and they give you a sense of who the person really is.

Often, it helps if you have things in common with the potential coach. For example, if they have kids and you have kids, there is common ground, and they can better understand your needs for accommodating your family.

I can tell you from experience it's easy to get lost in the transition between your old life and your new life. It can feel overwhelming and isolating. It's important to have some sort of support during this time. Otherwise, the path of least resistance turns out to be the one that brings you right back into your old patterns. I can't tell you how many times I thought, "I can just keep doing accounting work, and I'll be fine," when things got hard. It's almost like a default in our minds that resets us to stagnation mode.

Your subconscious is comfortable in the known and familiar territory. It will constantly try to get you back there, so it can relax and not do much work. Your subconscious is lazy! Your job is to keep pushing it out of its comfort zone. The more you do that, the more it will get used to this new way of thinking and behaving. Once you program it with enough new data, pushing the limits and trying new things will become the new default. And then, you'll automatically seek out new opportunities and areas for growth.

It takes time, but with the right support in place, you can accomplish wonderful things!

Celebrating Milestones

Your purpose is reflected in every aspect of your life. It's not just about work and career. When you are truly in your purpose, everything about you reflects it. From the way you interact with your kids to the way you handle your money, everything is impacted. When you notice yourself behaving and thinking authentically, you should celebrate yourself. Acknowledging a thought or behavior you'd like to repeat is reinforcement, programming the subconscious in that direction.

My favorite way to celebrate my success in aligning with my purpose is through journaling. (If you haven't noticed, journaling helps with any thought process or reprogramming! Highly recommend.) When you write out your wins, you take it from abstract to concrete. Words define the sense of accomplishment you're feeling, and you can better identify the associated emotions. By writing, you give yourself more praise in a more concrete way than you do by just thinking about the success. This elicits gratitude, which is essential for attracting more things to be grateful for.

When we simply think about our success without writing it down, we tend to think with a cloud of doubt over the accomplishment, like it's not really ours, or we downplay it for some reason. It's like we don't feel comfortable giving ourselves credit. When you write about your success, however, it tends to be more direct and the feeling of pride has a chance to shine through. Then, when you reread what you wrote, you get to feel that pride again.

This is why gratitude journaling is so potent. You have endless opportunities to tap into the gratitude you feel in a moment. I write my gratitude entries in my Purpose Journal, and before I do, I like to flip to a random page and reread an entry from a prior moment in my life. It's so nice to revisit things I was grateful for in the recent past. Most of them are ones I repeat some iteration of almost daily—kids, husband, freedom, work—but often I come across something unique.

A recent one from my RV trip reads:

Today I am grateful for the chance to share a piece of our history with the kids. We renewed our vows at the place we got married (A Little White Chapel in Vegas). Elvis serenaded us with the song I walked down the aisle to 9 years ago ("My Way," originally by Frank Sinatra, although Elvis did a cover). It was a dream come true to have my kids by my side as I re-vowed to love their father forever.

Gratitude attracts more abundance. It's a principle of the Law of Attraction, and it's something I've experienced firsthand. From a scientific perspective, it's all about the Reticular Activating System (RAS), which is a bundle of neurons in the brain. The RAS filters information your brain receives to help you focus on what's important. This is why sometimes we miss things in our environment, because the

RAS determined it wasn't important enough for the information to enter your awareness.

For example, when you're walking down the street, do you notice every blade of grass, every leaf, every flower? Even the most detail-oriented person can't do that. It's because your brain would be on information overload. Instead, your brain notices what's important—the angry dog running at you, your neighbor's new car, the Smiths finally mowed their damn lawn, etc.

The RAS is also the system behind manifestation and, I believe, the scientific explanation supporting the phenomenon. When you change your focus from negativity to positivity, from lack to abundance, and from brooding to gratitude, you begin to notice more things in your environment that support your new mindset. And then, confirmation bias jumps in to say, "See? I told you so!" but in a positive way this time. When this happens over and over again, the neural pathways that you've just laid with your shift in focus begin to strengthen, and positivity becomes second nature.

You might be thinking, *Okay, but how does a positive mindset influence my outcomes? It's the outcomes I'm interested in, Izabela!*

Same. So, here it is. When your perspective shifts, you begin to notice things differently. When you begin to think with gratitude, compassion, and abundance at the forefront, your thought process ends in a different place. For example, when you notice that the Smiths finally mowed their lawn, you might also notice that you haven't seen Mr. Smith in a few weeks, and now here he is, tinkering in his garage like he used to, so you spark a conversation and find out he's been sick for the last couple of months.

When you first noticed the mowed lawn from a place of judgment, that the Smith's lawn was making the neighborhood look less put-together, you missed the social connection with the person behind the issue. When you switched to a more positive disposition, you were able to dissect the judgment and see the human factor. In a very accelerated example, maybe your conversation with Mr. Smith resulted in you offering to help him around the yard, and then you get to talking and realize he's a secret billionaire who funds startups, and now you have the funding you've been looking for to start your business and live your purpose.

Of course, that's not totally realistic, but I'm trying to show you that an unexpected connection can lead to opportunities you never even considered. You would have totally missed that connection if you were focused on negativity and judgment, but when your mindset switched to compassion and gratitude, your RAS allowed you to notice the human factor in the unkempt lawn situation, and that human connection can lead to beautiful new things, because, ultimately, it's human connection that opens the doors for opportunity.

Gratitude is kind of like flipping a switch in your brain. It turns on your magnetic power for attracting the things you desire. You attract whatever you focus on, so even if things aren't perfect in your life, find something to be grateful for. You'll attract more things to be grateful for, and the progress compounds from there.

So, when you have a win on the journey toward your purpose, celebrate it. Call it out, point to it, draw internal attention toward it. I want to be clear, though. Your celebration can be externally quiet. I'm not saying you need to throw a party every time you make a glimmer of progress. In fact, quite the opposite. Celebrate yourself in your own internal world. Tell yourself how proud you are of the progress you've made, reward yourself with a sticker chart, treat yourself like a kindergartener who just remembered to wash their hands after using the bathroom.

Psychology says, when we are rewarded for something, we're very likely to repeat it. So, celebrate the small wins, and you will keep winning.

Final Reflections

If there is one thing that I've learned from my purpose journey and through writing this book, it's that progress is not linear, and it doesn't feel like progress in the moment. (That might be two things, actually.) Some days, you'll feel like you've conquered the world and have it all figured out. Other days, you feel like you're just getting by. When you're in the moment and you're not sure where to go next, I recommend journaling on it.

As I'm sure you're well aware by now, journaling has changed my life and given me an unprecedented clarity. In fact, I don't even know how I managed to get by before I started journaling, because I can't imagine my life without it now. It provides me the chance to really examine my thoughts, unfiltered.

As I mentioned, when we think, we work through a cloud of random thoughts and distractions. When we write, we have the chance to focus on the topic of concern and only that topic. The fleeting thoughts will still be there; and while you might get distracted for a moment, once the thoughts float on by, you can anchor back into the topic of your writing.

Rereading is even better, because you get to revisit a stream of consciousness and a version of you that no longer exists. Even if it was written just yesterday, you're a different person with different thoughts today. Sometimes, when I read back what I wrote, I think, *Wow, that was dramatic,* but in the moment when I was writing it, it was a really big deal for me. Sometimes, I even realize I'm being dramatic *while* I'm writing, and that's helpful for centering my thoughts and thinking more clearly.

As much as I like going back through my gratitude entries, my favorite part of journaling is going back and reading what I wrote during a difficult time in my life, so I can see the progress I've made. The progress was not obvious when it was happening, so it's helpful to go back and see it from the perspective of my past self. This helps me to celebrate my wins in a more concrete way, because I can compare who I am to who I was. Every version of myself is memorialized, and I revisit myself whenever I want. It's comforting, knowing I can do that.

For example, I love rereading the entries from my RV trip. I often found myself wondering if I was damaging my kids by keeping them confined in such tight quarters, and I worried about our safety on the road. Looking back and knowing that the trip was the best thing for our family, I feel silly for worrying. I just want to give that version of me a big hug and tell her to keep going. My family is now closer than ever, and my kids tell me all the time how much they miss RVing.

I hope journaling becomes as life-changing for you as it has for me. If you go through the purpose-seeking process valiantly and consistently, you will get to know yourself on a much deeper level. And you will probably want to keep exploring! You can do that by creating your own journal prompts as you get to know yourself better and by digging into certain facets of who you are and why.

I hope that the Purpose Activation Blueprint has provided you with clarity on who you are and where you are meant to go. You have the power within you to live your purpose. If you're called toward something, it's not random. It was placed upon your heart for a reason, and you are the only one who can execute it.

I invite you to step into your power and take control of your happiness and destiny with absolution and force. We don't have a lot of time here on Earth, and any moment wasted is a missed opportunity.

If you have an idea, take action on it. Ideas are formed from energy, and their purpose is to be brought into the world. They enter the minds of those who have the ability to birth them, but they do not wait around forever. If you've ever heard anyone say (or maybe you've experienced this yourself), "They stole my idea! I thought of that before it came out," it's because the idea was there, but action was not taken. So, the idea moved on to someone who *would* bring it to life.

The longer you wait to be ready, the longer you'll be waiting to be ready. There's no such thing as "ready." There's no grand invitation to step into your purpose, and you won't be enlightened as soon as you take the first step. I'm not going to lie to you and say it's going to be easy every step of the way. There will be challenges, you will ask yourself *WTF am I doing*, and there will be times when you want to quit and go back to normal and easy.

I promise you, though, it's so worth it. Do not quit. Do not give up. Keep pushing through the challenges and the fear and keep listening to your intuition. Your body knows the way, you just need to follow its instructions.

The opposite of empty feels good. It's energizing and flowy and calm. When you're living your purpose, even the hard times are not so bad, because you have something in your life that sparks joy, excitement, and, most importantly, peace.

Purpose gives you peace. It creates a sense of calm in your life, because you are exactly where you need to be. You no longer feel like you're falling behind or missing out. Even if people around you are excelling, making more money, or outpacing you in any way, it doesn't matter. The comparison doesn't exist anymore. You gain the ability to be happy for others without a twinge of envy. It's genuine and it's heartfelt, thus improving those relationships.

Finding your purpose is kind of like reaching the Buddhist state of enlightenment, but for work and occupation instead of absolute being. The peace that comes through aligning with your true desires and passions and the clarity that comes from intentional living and reflection feel like you're transcending the realm of suffering. You begin to truly look at things in a different way, and your decision-making becomes more intuitive. The resistance you once felt around your work and career falls away, and it begins to feel easy.

I would argue, in fact, that living with purpose is a step toward enlightenment. There is an element of trust in aligning with your purpose, because it requires you to take a step into the unknown and abandon what is considered "normal" and "safe." That trust is likely something you've never felt before, but I believe it is key to our liberation from attachment and suffering.

I've recently discovered that Buddhism aligns with many of my beliefs and practices. I was never able to put a label on my woo-woo belief system until now, and it turns out it's not as woo-woo as I'd thought. Instead, it's an entire philosophical tradition and spiritual movement, dating back to the fifth century BC, with adherents accounting for up to ten percent of the world population. So, I guess I'm in good company. This further reinforces my purpose and inspires me to get my message out into the world.

I'm not exactly sure how my purpose will unfold in the future, but I trust it will happen in a way that aligns with my highest good. I would argue that trust is the most important part of the Purpose Activation Blueprint. We've been socially conditioned to abandon trust in ourselves. So much so that the word *intuition*, itself, is perceived as something abstract and mystical, when, in reality, it's actually a real cognitive process that operates on pattern recognition, experience, and subconscious processing, and it can be tapped into by listening to your body.

I hope you have enjoyed getting to know yourself a little bit better. I believe you can do amazing things. All it takes is putting yourself first. As soon as you decide you want better, new things will enter. You need to let them in and see where they take you, even if they're unexpected. If you want different, you have to *be* different. Be the version of you who already has the things you want. Align with that, and watch as the opportunities your higher self attracts unfold before you, paving the way to the life you dream of.

Remember, you must remain open and explore every opportunity that crosses your path, when your intuition nudges you toward it. If you ignore them or shut them down because you're "not ready," they will stop showing up. Readiness is a mindset, not a circumstance. You can be *ready* at any time you choose. All it takes is a decision to explore new possibilities and pursue them when your intuition tells you to.

If your intuition is telling you to take the next step with me, I happily invite you to enter my world on a more intimate level. I have many options for you to explore that will help you step fully into your power and break through your limitations. Please visit themindfulwaypoint.com for more information and follow me on Instagram @izabela.oquendo.

I believe in your power. I believe you're capable. I believe in you.

In mindful alignment,

Izabela

SOURCE NOTES

Ipsos. *Global Happiness 2023: Life Satisfaction Across the World.* Ipsos, 2023, www.ipsos.com/en/global-happiness-2023.

Kahneman, D., & Deaton, A. (2010). *High income improves evaluation of life but not emotional well-being.* Proceedings of the National Academy of Sciences, 107(38).

Waldinger, R. J., & Schulz, M. S. (2023). *The Good Life: Lessons from the World's Longest Scientific Study of Happiness.* Simon & Schuster.

ACKNOWLEDGMENTS

I'M BEYOND GRATEFUL for the opportunity to share my thoughts and my story with you. This would not have been possible without my wonderful husband, John. He encouraged me to keep going when I felt like giving up, he inspired me when I didn't know what to say, and he held me when I processed heavy emotions that resulted from my work on the Purpose Activation Blueprint. He also kept the kids occupied when I needed to write. He is my rock and my best friend.

My kids, Luciana and Charlie, are the reason for all of this work. I want to show them that life is not passive. They have the ability to make whatever they want of themselves, and my only mission is to give them a life of freedom and empowerment. I know that starts with me and the example I set, and *that's* why I do bold and inspirational things—to show them it's possible, so they'll do even bigger things in their lives.

My publisher, Samatha Joy, and my writing coach, Raina O'Dell, have made this book possible. I started writing with no concrete plan as to how it would end up being released into the world, and they made it all happen. The vision and creativity these women possess is second to none, and I'm thankful they encouraged me to embrace the parts of me that I wanted to hide.

To my editor, Kathryn Galán–your insight, precision, and patience for all my last-minute edits helped shape these pages into something I'm proud to share with the world. Thank you for honoring my message and helping it land with clarity and grace.

And finally, thank you, reader, for listening to what I have to say. This is all for you, and I hope at least some part of your life is better after reading this book. You are the reason I do what I do, and my purpose is to serve you.

ABOUT THE AUTHOR

IZABELA OQUENDO IS A mental health professional, speaker, and transformation coach who takes a grounded yet expansive approach to manifestation by using mindfulness. Having tried on many hats in her career and after building multiple successful businesses, she chose a radically different path focused on travel, family, and purpose.

Today, she empowers women to break free from fear, trust their inner voice, and build lives rooted in boldness, clarity, and joy. Through her signature programs and writing, Izabela guides her readers inward to reconnect with their purpose, rewire limiting beliefs, and manifest from a place of surrender and presence.

She is the creator of the Purpose Activation Blueprint, a guided framework designed to help readers discover their soul-aligned path, and she is the founder of The Mindful Waypoint, a platform and movement dedicated to helping women release fear and manifest success through alignment. When she is not writing or coaching, you'll find her with her husband and children, living the life she once dreamed of by the sea in Spain.

www.ingramcontent.com/pod-product-compliance
Lightning Source LLC
LaVergne TN
LVHW011416080426
835512LV00005B/95